FINANCIAL MANAGEMENT AFTER GLOBALIZATION

FINANCIAL MANAGEMENT AFTER GLOBALIZATION

By

Rabi N. Misra

&

G. Chandraya

DISCOVERY PUBLISHING HOUSE PVT. LTD.

NEW DELHI-110 002

Published by:
Tilak Wasan

DISCOVERY PUBLISHING HOUSE PVT. LTD.
4383/4B, Ansari Road, Darya Ganj
New Delhi-110 002 (India)
Phone : +91-11-23279245, 23253475, 43596065
E-mail : discoverybooksindia@gmail.com
discoverypublishinghouse@gmail.com
web : www.discoverypublishinggroup.com

***Reprinted:* 2019**

***First Published:* 2011**

ISBN: 978-81-8356-711-4

Financial Management After Globalization

Printed at:
Infinity Imaging Systems
Delhi

Preface

Financial Management is that part of Managerial activity which is concerned with the planning, controlling of Financial resources of an Organization. The subject Financial management is of immense value for the students of finance as well as to the financial managers of different organizations. Among the various decisions taken by an organization, financial decisions are the most important and vital. Most financial decisions, such as the purchase of assets or procurement of funds, affect firms' cash flows in different time period. The time value of money and risk, need due consideration in financial decision-making. The owners would be maximized when wealth or net present value is created for making a financial decision. Net Present Value (NPV) of a financial decision is the difference between the present value of cash inflows and present value of cash outflows. After globalization, financial management need due consideration. The financial manager has to tackle the financial decisions as "Glass with Care". This book has focussed the different issues and solutions which are generally faced by financial managers at different times. It will also help the managers who are dealing with financial matters and to the students of management and others for taking financial decisions.

Dr. R.N. Misra
Mr. G. Chandrayya

Acknowledgement

We are very much thankful to Smt. Swarana Prava Misra, Smt. Amrita Rani Misra, Lecturer in English, Rookesh Kumar Misra, HR Manager for their kind help, cooperation and encouragement in writing this book.

We also express our sincere gratitude to Mr. Tilak Wasan, the Director Discovery Publishing House Pvt. Ltd., Ansari Road, Darya Ganj, New Delhi for his positive attitude in publishing this book. We are also thankful to his son Parul, and all staff members of Discovery Publishing House for their kind help and co-operation in publishing this book.

Dr. Rabi N. Misra
Mr. G. Chandrayya

Contents

of Replacement Situation—Cash Flow Estimation—Working Capital Effect—Incremental Analysis—Investment Evaluation Techniques (or) Capital Budgeting Techniques—Non-discounted Cash Flow Criteria/Traditional Techniques—Pay Back Period (Non-Uniform Cash Flows)—PBP (Uniform Cash Flows)—Accounting Rate of Return (ARR)—Merits—Demerits—Decision Rule—ARR (Non Uniform Profits)—ARR (Uniform Profits with Salvage Value a Working Capital)—Discounted Cash Flow (PCF) Criteria/Modern Techniques—Discounted Payback Period (DPBP)—Decision Rule—Net Present Value—NPV (Non-Uniform Cash Flows)—A Case of Conventional Project—Calculation of NPV—NPV (Uniform Cash Flows): A Case of Non-Conventional Project—Internal Rate of Return—Merits—Demerits—Decision Rule—IRR (Uniform Cash Flows)—Profitability Index (PI) or Benefit – Cost Ratio (B/C Ratio)—Decision Rule—NPV 1RR Is Methods—A Comparison—NPV and IRR.Similarities—Incremental IRR—NPV and IRR Methods: Differences—Conclusion Over DCF Techniques—Illustrations—Calculation of IRR—Calculation of NPV—Capital Budgeting, Risk and Uncertainty—Assumptions of Capital Budgeting Under Risk—Uncertainty Risk and Certainly—Types of Risks—Risk in Capital Budgeting Analysis—Conventional Techniques—Risk Adjusted Discount Rate (RADR)—Advantages of RADR—Limitations of RADR—Advantages—Limitation—Statistical Techniques—Probability Distributiion Approach—Evaluation of Proposals—Capital Budgeting Decisions Under Capital Rationing—Capital Rationing is of two Types

CHAPTER 1 The Finance Function

Introduction

The term 'nature' as applied to financial management refers to its relationship with the closely-related fields of economics and accounting, its functions, scope and objectives. Financial management, as an academic discipline, has undergone fundamental changes in its scope and coverage. In the early years of its evolution it was treated synonymously with the rising of funds. In the current literature pertaining to financial management, a broader scope so as to include, in addition to procurement of funds, efficient use of resources is universally recognized.

Finance and Related Discipline

Financial management is that managerial activity which is concerned with the planning and controlling of the firm's financial resources. Though it was a branch of economics till 1890, as a separate activity or discipline it is of recent origin.

Finance and Economics

The relevance of economics to financial management can be described in the light of the two broad areas of economics: macroeconomics and microeconomics.

Macroeconomics is concerned with the institutional structure of the banking system, money and capital markets, financial intermediaries, monetary, credit and fiscal policies and economic policies dealing with, and controlling level of, activity within an economy.

Microeconomics concerns with the determination of optimal strategies of effective operations of business firms.

Thus, knowledge of economics is necessary for a financial manager to understand both the financial environment and the decision theories, which underlie contemporary financial management.

Finance and Accounting

Finance and accounting functions are closely related.

The-primary objective of accounting is to measure the performance of the firm, assess its financial condition, and determine the base for tax payment. The principal goal of financial management is to create shareholder value by investing in profitable projects and minimizing the cost of financing.

The accounting reports are based on actual concept while the focus of financial decisions is based on cash flows particularly the magnitude, Liming and risk of cash flows being the fundamental determinants of value.

Finance and Production

The production department in any firm is concerned with provision of production facilities, production cycle, skilled and unskilled labour, storage of finished goods, capacity utilization etc. The financial management has a useful role to play in interaction with the production management as the cost of production assumes a substantial portion of the total cost.

Financial and HRM

The personnel department has to work with the finance manager while evaluating different schemes of training programmes, employees welfare, economy in manpower, computerization, incentives schemes, revision of pay scales etc. The best possible option should be identified keeping in view both the employee's welfare and the interest of the firm. Considering the financial implications of all these decisions is an important dimension.

Finance and Marketing

The marketing department is entrusted with the responsibility of framing marketing, selling, advertisement and other related policies to achieve the sales target. It is also required to frame credit and collection policies to maintain and increase the market share, creating a brand name, to acquire a competitive edge etc. The finance manager has to play an active role in interaction with the marketing department in the process of these decisions.

The financial implications of the proposed advertisement policy, price-war manoeuvres, liberalization of credit policy etc. must be critically analyzed before these are adopted and implemented.

Conclusion: Financial management is closely linked with different functional areas of management. Since financial management is involved in overall planning and control of funds of the entire firm, it is related to each and every segment of operations of the firms. The efforts of all the departments should be directed towards achieving the objectives of the organizations.

Scope of Financial Management

Financial management emerged as a distinct field of study at the turn of the 20th century. Its evolution may be divided into two broad phases: (*i*) the traditional phase, and (*ii*) the modern phase.

(*i*) Traditional Approach *(Outsider-looking-in Approach)*

The traditional approach to the scope of the finance function evolved during the 1920s and 1930s and dominated academic thinking during the forties and through the early fifties.

The scope of the finance function' was treated by the traditional approach in the narrow sense of procurement of funds by corporate enterprise to meet their financing needs. The term 'procurement' was used in a broad sense so as to — include the whole gamut of raising funds externally. Thus defined, the field of study dealing with finance was treated as encompassing three interrelated aspects of raising and administering resources from outside.

The focus of financial management was mainly on certain episodic events or frequent happenings like formation, issuance of capital, major expansion, merger, reorganization, and liquidation in the life cycle of the firm.

The approach was mainly descriptive and institutional. The instruments of financing, the institutions and procedures used in capital markets, and the legal aspects of financial events formed the core of financial management.

CRITICISMS

1. The traditional treatment of finance was criticized for its emphasis on issues relating to the procurement of funds by corporate enterprises, the finance function was equated with the issues involved in raising and administering funds.
2. The focus was on financing problems of corporate enterprises. To that extent the scope of financial management was confined only to a segment of the industrial enterprises, as non-corporate organizations lay outside its scope.
3. The treatment was around episodic events, such as promotion, incorporation, merger, consolidation, reorganizations and so on. Financial management was confined to a description of these infrequent happenings in the life of an enterprise ignoring the day-to-day financial problems of a company.

4. The outsiders point of view was dominant. Financial management was viewed mainly from the point of view of the investment bankers, lenders, and other outside interests.

Traditional approach confined financial management to issues involved in procurement of external funds, it did not consider the important dimension of allocation of capital.

(*ii*) Modem Approach *(Insider-looking-out Approach)*

The modern phase began in the mid 1950s and has witnessed an accelerated pace of development with the infusion of ideas from economic theory and application of, quantitative methods of analysis.

The modern approach provides a solution to the above shortcomings. The finance function covers both acquisition of funds as well as their allocations. Thus, apart from the issues involved in acquiring external funds, the main concern of financial management is the efficient and wise allocation of funds to various uses.

The Distinctive Features of the Modern Phase

1. The central concern of financial management is considered to be a rational matching of funds to their uses so as to maximize the wealth of current shareholders.
2. The approach of financial management has become more analytical and quantitative.

Since the beginning of the modern phase many significant and seminal developments have occurred in the fields of capital budgeting, capital structure theory, efficient-market theory, option pricing theory, agency theory, arbitrage pricing theory, valuation models, dividend policy, working capital management, financial modelling, and behavioural finance. Many more exciting developments are in the store making finance a fascinating and challenging field.

Finance Decisions

The finance manager's role is broadened with the change in the perspective of financial management. A finance manager should make decisions considering issues like

(*i*) How large should an enterprise be, and how fast should it grow ?

(*ii*) In what form should it hold assets ? and

(*iii*) What should be the composition of its liabilities ?

The solution to three major problems correspond major decisions as functions of finance:

(*i*) The investment decision;

(*ii*) The financing decision; and

(*iii*) The dividend policy decision.

The functions of raising funds, investing them in assets and distributing returns earned from assets to shareholders are respectively known as financing, investment and dividend decisions. While performing these functions, a firm attempts to balance cash inflows and outflows. This is called liquidity decision. Finance functions or decisions include :

1. Investment or long-term asset-mix decision;
2. Financing or capital-mix decision;
3. Dividend or profit allocation decision;
4. Liquidity or short-term asset-mix decision.

1. **Investment Decision:** The investment decision relates to the selection of assets in which funds will be invested by a firm. The assets which can be acquired fall into two broad groups: (*i*) long term assets which yield a return over a period of time in future, (*ii*) short-term or current assets, defined as those assets which in the normal course of business are convertible into cash without diminution in value, 'usually within a year.

The first of these involving the first category of assets is popularly known in financial literature as capital budgeting. The aspect of financial decision-making with reference to current assets or short-term assets is popularly termed as working capital management.

2. **Financing Decision:** The concern of the financing decision is with the financing-mix or capital structure or leverage. The term capital structure refers to the proportion of debt (fixed-interest sources of financing) and equity capital (variable-dividend securities/sources of funds). The financing decision of a firm relates to the choice of the proportion of these sources to finance the investment requirements. A proper balance between debt and equity to ensure a trade-off between risk and return to the shareholders is necessary.
3. **Dividend Policy Decision:** Another decision of financial management is the decision relating to the dividend policy. The dividend should be analyzed in relation to the financing decision of a firm. The firms can distribute returns to the shareholders in the form of dividends or can be retained in the business itself, the decision as to which course should be followed depends largely on a significant element in the dividend decision, the dividend payout ratio i.e., what proportion of net profits should be paid out to the shareholders considering the investment opportunities available within the firm.
4. **Working Capital Management:** It refers to the management of current assets and current liabilities. A firm should have adequate working capital. It should invest sufficiently in current assets and have the ability to meet its current obligations to avoid the risk of bankruptcy. Current assets should be efficiently managed so that neither inadequate nor unnecessary funds are locked up. The key strategies and considerations in ensuring a trade off between profitability and

liquidity is important dimension of working capital management.

To conclude the traditional approach had a very narrow perception. The modern approach has broadened the scope of financial management. Three major decisions, namely, investment, financing and dividend are interrelated and should be jointly taken so that financial decision-making is optimal and are in relation to the objectives of financial management.

Role of Finance Manager

A financial manager is a person who is responsible in a significant way to carry out the finance functions. The financial manager occupies a key position responsible for shaping the fortunes of the enterprise, and is involved in the most vital decision of the allocation of capital needs to have a broader and far-sighted outlook, and must ensure that the funds of the enterprise are utilized in the most efficient manner. The finance manager's actions have far-reaching consequences for the firm because they influence the size, profitability, growth, risk and survival of the firm, and as a consequence, affect the overall value of the firm. The financial manager, therefore, must have a clear understanding and a strong grasp of the nature and scope of the finance functions.

Raising of funds during the major events, such as promotion, reorganization, expansion or diversification and day-to-day activities.

Efficient and effective use of funds — Efficient allocation of funds — Understanding capital markets and — Profit planning.

A firm performs finance functions simultaneously and continuously in the normal course of the business. Finance functions call for skilful planning, control and execution of a firm's activities.

Thus while performing the finance functions, the financial manager should strive to maximize the market value of shares.

Profit Maximization Decision Criterion

According to this approach, actions that increase profits should be undertaken and those that decrease profits are to be avoided. In specific operational terms, as applicable to financial management, the profit maximization criterion implies that the investment, financing and dividend policy decisions of a firm should be oriented to the maximization of profits. Profitability maximization would imply that a firm should be guided in financial decision-making by one test; select assets, projects and decisions which are profitable and reject those which are not. It provides the yardstick by which economic performance can be judged. Moreover, it leads to efficient allocation of resources, as resources tend to be directed to uses, which in terms of profitability are the most desirable. Finally, it ensures maximum social welfare.

Criticism

1. Profit maximization fails to serve as an operational criterion for maximizing the owner's economic welfare.
2. It fails to provide an operationally feasible measure for ranking alternative course of action in terms of their economic efficiency.
3. The definition of profit is ambiguous as it can be referred to profit before tax, total operating profit or total profit or profit per share.
4. It ignores the time value of money and does not make a distinction between returns received in different time periods.
5. It ignores risk. The streams of benefits may possess different degree of certainty leading to uncertainty of returns.

To conclude, the profit maximization criterion is inappropriate and unsuitable as an operational objective of investment, financing and dividend decisions of a firm. It is not only vague and ambiguous but it also ignores two important dimensions of financial analysis, namely, risk, and time value of money. It follows from the above that an appropriate operational decision criterion for financial management should (*i*) be precise and exact; (*ii*) be based on the *'bigger the* better' principle; (*iii*) Consider both quantity and quality dimensions of benefits; and (*iv*) recognize the time value of money. The alternative to profit maximization, that is, wealth maximization is one such measure.

Wealth Maximization Decision Criterion

This is also known as value maximization and is universally accepted as an appropriate operational decision criterion for financial management decisions as it is free of the limitations which characterize the profit maximization criterion. Its feature satisfy all the three requirements exactness, quality of benefits and the time value of money.

1. Based on the concept of cash flows than accounting profit. Measuring benefits in terms of cash flows avoids the ambiguity associated with accounting profits.
2. Considers both the quantity and quality dimensions of benefits and also incorporates the time value of money.

The implication of the uncertainty and timing dimensions of the benefits emanating from a financial decision is that adjustments should be made in the cashflow pattern to incorporate risk and to make an allowance for differences in the timing of benefits. The value of a stream of cash flows with value maximization criterion is calculated by discounting its element back to the present at a capitalization rate that reflects both time and risk.

The value maximization is an extension of profit maximization where value maximization decision criterion considers the time value of money, handling of the risk as measured by the uncertainty of the expected benefits. It is a precise and unambiguous concept, and therefore, an appropriate and feasible decision criterion for financial management decisions.

For the above reasons, the net present value maximization is superior to the profit maximization as an operational objective.

Risk Return Trade off

The financial decisions of the firm are interrelated and jointly affect the market value of its shares by influencing return and risk of the firm. The relationship between return and risk can be expressed as follows :

- Return = Risk free rate + Risk premium

Risk-free rate is compensation for time and risk premium for risk. A proper balance between risk and return should be maintained to maximize the market value of firms shares. This balance is known as risk • return trade off and every decision involve risk-return trade off. The interrelationship between market value, financial decisions and risk-return trade off is shown as below:

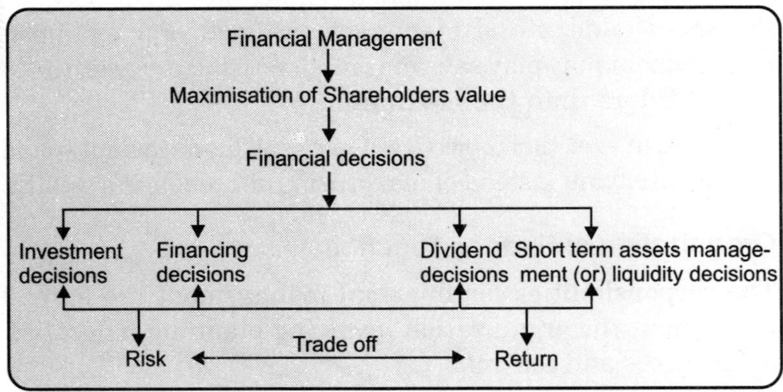

Conflict of Goal Between Management and Owners: Agency Problem

A feature of corporate enterprise is the separation of ownership and management where the management enjoys substantial autonomy in regard to the affairs of the firm. Shareholders hardly exercise any controlling influence on management as they are scattered and ill organised which makes the management to act in their interests rather than those of the owners.

Managers are the agents of share holders. There is often a lack of congruence in the objectives of the shareholders and managers, those leads to agency costs which represents loss in the value of the firm.

However, shareholders as owners of the enterprise have the right to change the management. Due to the threat of being dilodged/dismissed for poor performance, the management would have a natural inclination to achieve a minimum acceptable level of performance to satisfy the shareholder's requirements/goals, while focussing primarily on their own personal goals.

The wealth maximization objective may be in harmony with the interests of owner, employees, creditors and society, and be consistent with the management objective. There can, however, arise situations where a conflict may occur between the shareholder's and management's goal. For example, management may play safe and create satisfactory wealth for shareholders than the maximum.

Thus, in view their objective of survival, management would aim at satisfying instead of maximizing shareholder's wealth.

Organization of Finance Function

The responsibilities for financial management are spread throughout the organization involving planning, allocation of resources and control.

The ultimate responsibility for carrying out financial management functions lies with the top management. The financial management function differs, from firm to firm depending upon factors such as size of the firm, nature of its business, type of financing operations, ability of financial officers and the financial philosophy, and so on. Similarly, the designation of the chief executive of the finance department also differs widely in case of different firms. In some cases, they are known as finance managers while in others as vice-president (finance), director (finance), and financial controller and so on who reports directly to the top management. Managers such as controller and treasurer head various sections within the financial management area.

The following figure depicts the organization of the financial management function in a large typical firm.

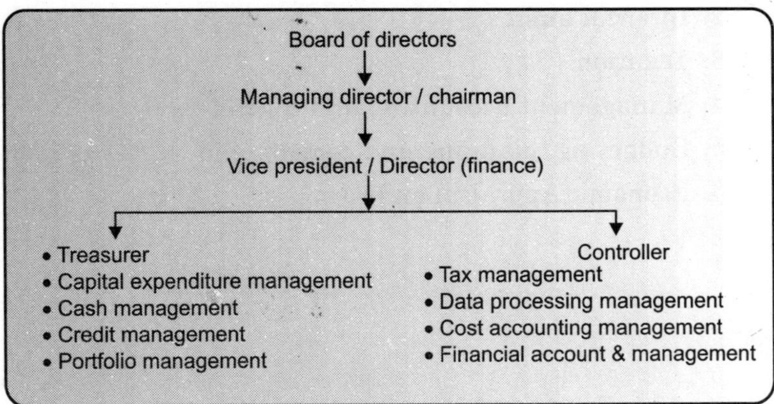

The job of the chief financial executive does not cover only routine aspects of finance and accounting.

As a member of the top management, he is closely associated with formulation of policies as well as decision making who heads the controllers and treasures. Their functions are described below.

The main concern of the treasurer is with the financing activities of the firm. Included in the range of his functions are :

1. Obtaining finance
2. Banking relationship
3. Investor relationship
4. Short-term financing
5. Cash management

6. Credit administration
7. Investments, and
8. Insurance.

The functions of the controller are related mainly to accounting and control. The typical functions performed by him include:

1. Financial accounting
2. Internal audit
3. Taxation
4. Management accounting and control
5. Budgeting, planning and control, and
6. Economic Appraisal and so on.

CHAPTER

2

Investment Decisions

A. WORKING CAPITAL MANAGEMENT

Concept of Project and Project Development Cycle

A project is a productive activity which can be analyzed, appraised and monitored independently.

A project may be defined as a scientifically evolved work plan devised to achieve a specific objective with a specified period of time. The three basic attributes area course of action, specific objectives and definite time perspective.

Characteristics of a Project

Though various connotation have been given to the concept of a project, they have four basic characteristics:

1. Investment pattern;
2. Benefits or gains;
3. Time limit; and
4. Location.

In short, *"the project is an economic activity with well-defined objectives and having a specific beginning and end"*. It should be amenable to planning, financing and implementation as a unit where both costs and returns are measurable.

Phase of Project Development Cycle

Project development cycle consists of three main stages :

1. The Pre-investment Phase :
   (*a*) Identifying of investment opportunity.
   (*b*) Preliminary project analysis
   (*c*) Feasibility study
   (*d*) Decision-making
2. The Implementation Phase
3. The Operational Phase

1. **Pre-Investment Phase:** This is the first stop in project development cycle and involves 4 aspects.

(*a*) *Identifying of Investment Opportunity :* Good projects are key to success and requires analysis of performance of existing industries, inputs and output analysis, review of import, exports, Government and financial institutions guidelines, analyze economic and social trends, new technological development etc.

(*b*) *Preliminary Project Analysis :* There are 5 important facets of project analysis:

(*i*) *Market Analysis;* To know the demand, market share of the proposed project under appraised where market analysis require wide information to use appropriate forecasting methods.

(*ii*) *Technical Analysis:* Involves analysis of engineering aspects of project. Technical analysis seeks to determine whether the prerequisites for the successful commissioning of the project have been considered and reasonably good chores have been made with respect to location, size, process, scale of operations, availability of raw materials etc.

(*iii*) *Financial Analysis:* Seeks to ascertain the financial viability of the project in terms of debt burden, satisfying return expectations, cost of capital, means of financing, level of risk etc.

(iv) *Economic Analysis:* Is also referred to social cost benefit analysis probing into economic benefits, costs impact of project on savings and investment, distribution of income in the society. Contribution of project towards employment, social orders etc.

(v) *Ecological Analysis:* To evaluate ecological implications for major projects like power plants, irrigation schemes, environment polluting industries etc., in terms of damage caused by the project to the environment and cost of restoration measures.

(c) *Feasibility Study:* The feasibility study is concerned with project generation analysis, evaluation and selection aspects of capital budgeting and involves the preliminary project analysis.

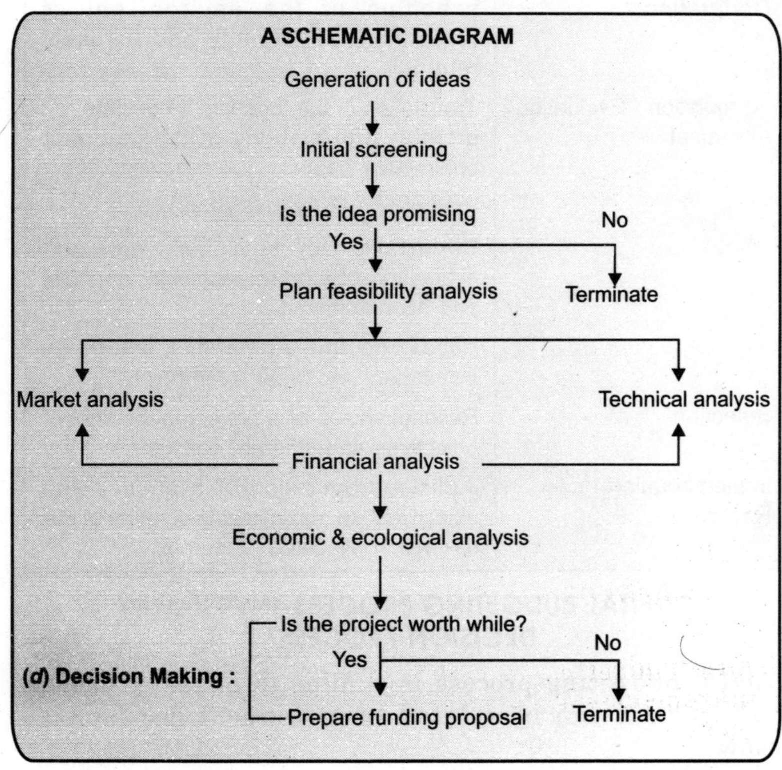

2. **The Implementation Phase:** This phase focuses on developing infrastructure for the commencement of project.
3. **The Operational Phase:** This phase focuses on manufacturing and production activity.

A project is a scheme of investing resources in an enterprise. An entrepreneur has to consider carefully various factors from the start to the finish in converting profitable opportunities into realities. The process of project management may be divided into six broad phases-identification, formulation, appraisal, selection, implementation, and management of projects.

Phase	Requirement
Identification/ Generation	Selection of a project after a careful scanning of the environment of investment opportunity and its likely return.
Formulation / Evaluation Appraisal	Translation of the Idea into a concrete project with scrutiny of Its important preliminary aspects.
	Preparation of feasibility reports.
	Undertake scrutiny, analysis and evaluation of market, technical, financial and economic variables.
	Assessing the profitability, return on Investment and break even points.
Selection	Rational choice of a project In the light of objectives and inherent constraints.
Implementation and Review	Judicious operation of a project with objectives like maximization of return at low risk within allocated resources.

CAPITAL BUDGETING PROCESS/INVESTMENT DECISION PROCESS

Capital budgeting process is similar to phase of project management can be related to investment decisions as below:

- Identification of potential investment opportunities.
- Assembling of proposal investments.
- Decision-making.
- Preparation of capital budget and appropriations.
- Implementation, and
- Performance review.

Thus *technically capital budgeting involves,*

- Generating investment project proposals consistent with the firm's strategic objectives.
- Estimating after - tax incremental operating cash flows for investment projects.
- Evaluating project incremental cash flows.
- Selecting projects based on a value-maximizing acceptance criterion.
- Reevaluating implemented investment projects continually and performing postauditis for completed projects.

Capital Budgeting

Introduction: "Capital Budgeting is *the process of evaluating and selecting long term investments that are consistent with the goal of shareholders wealth maximization".*

They involve current outlay for future returns over a long period of time. The term capital budgeting is also used as long term investment decisions or management of fixed assets.

Features

The following are the features of investment decisions:

- The exchange of current funds for future benefits.
- The funds are invested in long-term assets.
- The future benefits will occur to the firm over a series of years.

It is significant to emphasize that expenditures and benefits of an investment should be measured in cash. In the investment analysis, it is cash flow which is important, not the accounting profit. It may also be pointed out that investment decisions affect the firm's value. The firm's value will increase if investments are profitable and add to the shareholder's wealth. Thus, investment should be evaluated on the basis of a criterion which is compatible with the objective of the shareholder's wealth maximization.

Rationale

The rationale underlying the capital budgeting decision is efficiency. Thus, a firm must replace worn and obsolete plants and machinery, acquire fixed assets for current and new products and make strategic investment decisions. To achieve its objective of maximizing profits either by way of increased revenues or cost reductions. Capital budgeting decision can be of two types : (i) those which expand revenues; and (ii) those which reduce costs.

Investment Decisions Affecting Revenues: Such investment decisions are expected to bring in additional revenue, thereby raising the size of the firm's total revenue. They can be the result of either expansion of present operations or the development of new product lines. Both types of investment decisions involve acquisition of new fixed assets and are income-expansionary in nature in the case of manufacturing firms.

Investment Decisions Reducing Costs: Such decisions, by reducing costs, add to the total earnings of the firm. A classic example of such investment decisions are the replacement proposals when an asset warns out or becomes outdated. The firm must decide whether to continue with the existing assets or replace them. The firm evaluates the benefits from the new machine in terms of lower operating cost and the outlay that would be needed to replace the machine. Cost reduction investment decisions are subject to less uncertainty when compared to revenue increasing investment decisions.

Importance of Investment Decisions

Investment decisions require special attention because of the following reasons :

- They influence the firm's growth in the long run.
- They affect the risk of the firm
- They involve commitment of large amount of funds.
- They are irreversible, or reversible at substantial loss.
- They are among the most difficult decisions to make.

Growth: The effects of investment decisions extend into the future and have to be endured for a longer period than the consequences of the current operating expenditure. A firm's decision to invest in long-term assets has a decisive influence on the rate and direction of its growth. A wrong decision can prove disastrous for the continued survival of the firm; unwanted or unprofitable expansion of assets will result in heavy operating costs to the firm. On the other hand, inadequate investment in assets would make it difficult for the firm to compete successfully and maintain its market share.

Risk: A long-term commitment of funds may also change the risk complexity of the firm. If the adoption of an investment increases average gain but causes frequent fluctuations in its earnings, the firm will become more risky. Thus, investment decisions shape the basic character of a firm.

Funding: Investment decisions generally involve large amount of funds which make it imperative for the firm to plan its investment programmes very carefully and make an advance arrangement for procuring finances internally or externally.

Irreversibility: Most investment decisions are irreversible. It is difficult to find a market for such capital items once they have been acquired. The firm will incur heavy losses if such assets are scrapped.

Classification of Projects

Projects may be classified into one of the five categories:

1. New products of expansion of existing products
2. Replacement projects.
3. Research : Development
4. Exploration
5. Any other long-term projects.

Yet another useful way to classify investments is as follows :

1. Mutually exclusive investments.
2. Independent investments.
3. Contingent investments.

1. **Mutually Exclusive Investments:** Mutually exclusive investments serve the same purpose and compete with each other. If one investment is undertaken, others will have to be excluded. A company may, for example, either use a more labour-intensive, semi-automatic machine, or employ a more capital-investitive, highly automatic machine for production. Choosing the semi-automatic machine precludes the acceptance of the highly automatic machine.
2. **Independent Investments:** Independent investments serve different purposes and do not compete with each other. For example, a heavy engineering company may be considering expansion of its plant capacity to manufacture additional excavators and addition of new production facilities to manufacture a new product - light commercial vehicles. Depending on their profitability and availability of funds, the company can undertake both investments.

3. **Contigent Investments:** These are dependent projects, the choice of one investment necessitates undertaking one or more other investments.

To understand the evaluation of investment projects, one should understand the important concept i.e.,

TIME VALUE OF MONEY

Time Value of Money

The value of a unit of money is different in different time periods. The value of a sum of money received today is more than its value received offer sometime, i.e., present value of rupee is worth more than that of future and hence can also be referred to as time preference for money.

Techniques

In order to have logical and meaningful comparisons between cash flows that result in different time periods. It is necessary to convert the sums of money to a common point of time. There are two techniques involved.

1. Compounding technique.
2. Discounting technique.

1. Compounding Technique: The amount of interest earned on principal (initial deposit) will become part of principal and interest gets compounded.

For *example*: X invests in savings bank account of Rs. 1000 at 5% interest.

Annual Compounding

Particulars	Year (n)		
	1	2	3
Principal Amt (p)	1,000	1,050	1102.5
Interest rate (i)	0,05	0.05	0.05
Amt. of interest	50.00	52.50	55.125
Ending principal (A)	1,050	1,102.50	1,157.625

The compound procedure can be calculated by using the following equation :

$$A = p(1 + i)^n$$
$$= 1000\ (1.05)^3 = 1{,}157.625$$

2. Discounting Technique or Present Value : The concept of present value is the exact opposite to that of compound value.

Present value is the current value of a future amount. The amount to be invested today at a given interest rate over a specified period to equal the future amount. Discounting is determining the present value of a future amount.

From the compounding formula $A = P\ (1 + l)^n$

In this case i = Compound rate

Present value equation :

$$P = \frac{A}{(1+l)^n} = A\left\{\frac{1}{(1+l)^n}\right\} = A\ (PVIF)$$

here i = discount rate

PVIF = Present value interest factor (A-3 table). To know how much should be invested to earn 1060 at 6% one year from now.

Using present value equation we get = $\frac{1060}{1.06} = 1000$

Using PVIF from A - 3 tables at 6% for 1 year

we get = 1060 (0.943) = 999.99 = 1000

In other words 1/1.06 = 0.943 [PVIF given in A-3 tables]

Present Value of Series of Cash Flows

The present value of a cash flow stream — uneven or even — may be calculated with the help of the following formula :

$$PV_n = \frac{A_1}{(1+i)} + \frac{A_2}{(1+i)^2} + ... + \frac{A_n}{(1+i)^n} = \sum_{i=1}^{n} \frac{A_t}{(1+i)^t}$$

where PV_n = present value of a cash flow stream

A_t – cash flow occurring at the end of year t

r = discount rate

n = duration of the cash flow stream

Calculation of the present value of an uneven cash flow stream, using a discount rate of 12 per cent.

(*a*) Present Value of an Uneven Cash Flow Stream:

Year	Cash Flow Rs.	$PIVF_{12\times>n}$	Present Value of Individual Cash flow
1	1,000	0.893	893
2	2,000	0.797	1,594
3	2,000	0,712	1,424
4	3,000	0.636	1,908 .
5	3,000	0.567	1,701
6	4,000	0.507	2,028
7	4,000	0.452	1,808
8	5,000	0.404	2,020
Present value of the cash flow stream			13,376

(*b*) Present Value of Even Cash Flow Stream: The calculation becomes simple in case of even cash flows. We use the concept of annuity. Annuity: is a stream of equal annual cash flows. The cumulative of PVIF is given as annuity. Table A-4 gives annuity values. Consider the following example:

Mr. X will earn cash inflows of 1,000 for 5 years and the rate of interest he can earn from his investment is 10%.

Long Method for Finding Present Value of an Annuity of Rs. 1,000 for Five Years

Year End 1	Cash Flows 2	Present Value Factor 3	Present Value (2) x (3) 4
1	Rs. 1,000	0.909	Rs. 909.00
2	1,000	0.826	826.00
3	1,000	0.751	751.00
4	1,000	0.683	683.00
5	1,000	0.621	621.00
			3,790.00

Simplifying the equation by taking out 1,000 as common factor outside the equation, P = Rs. 1,000 (0.999 + 0.826 + 0.751 + 0.683 + 0.621) = Rs 1,000 (3.790) – Rs. 3,790

Thus the present value of an annuity can be found by multiplying the annuity amount by the, sum of the present value factors for each year of the life of the annuity. Such readymade calculations are available in Table T-4.

The generalized formula to calculate the present value of an annuity :

$$P = \frac{A_1}{(1+i)} + \frac{A_2}{(1+i)^2} + \frac{A_3}{(1+i)^3} \ldots\ldots + \frac{A_n}{(1+i)^n}$$

$$= A\left\{\frac{1}{(1+i)} + \frac{1}{(1+i)^2} + \frac{1}{(1+i)^3} + \ldots\ldots \frac{1}{(1+t)^n}\right\}$$

$$= A\left\{\sum_{t=1}^{n} \frac{1}{(1+i)^2}\right\}$$

i.e., $PV = A$ (Annuity discount factor)

Investment Evaluation Criteria

The following characteristics should be possessed by a sound investment evaluation criterion:

- It should consider all cash flows to determine the true profitability of the project.
- It should provide for an objective and unambiguous way of separating good projects from bad projects.
- It should help ranking of projects according to their true profitability.
- It should recognize the fact that bigger cash flows are preferable to smaller ones and early cash flows are preferable to later ones.
- It should help to choose among mutually, exclusive projects that project which maximizes the shareholder's wealth.

Data Requirement: Identifying Relevant Cash Flows

Cash Flows vs Accounting Profit

Capital budgeting is concerned with investment decisions which yield return over a period of time in future. The foremost requirement for evaluation of any capital investment proposal is to estimate the future benefits accruing from the investment proposal. Theoretically, two alternative criteria are available to quantify the benefits; (*i*) accounting profit, and (*ii*) cash flows.

The following are the differences between cash flows and accounting profits.

S.No.	Cash Flow	Accounting Profit
1.	It doesn't consider non-cash expenses.	Consider non-cash expenses
2.	Cash flows reflect actual cash transactions associated with the project.	Accounting treatment doesn't reflect the original need for cash.
3.	Considers time value of money.	Ignores time value of money.
4.	Cash flows are quiet useful for decision criteria.	Accounting profit is quiet useful as performance measures.

Accounting profit is adjusted for non-cash expenditure to determine actual cash-inflows Hence the cash flow approach of measuring future benefits of a project is superior to accounting approach, which can be clearly understood by the table depicted below.

A Comparison of Cash Flow and Accounting Profit Approaches

Accounting Approach Towards Benefits Revenues			Cash Flow Approach Towards 'Benefits'	
	Rs. 1,000			Rs. 1,000
Less : Expenses :				
Cash expenses	Rs. 500		Rs. 500	
Depreciation	300	800		
Earnings before tax		200		
Tax (0.35)		70	70	570
Net earnings after taxes/cash flow		130		430

The above table shows that the accounting profits amounting to Rs. 130 are less than . the cash flow (Rs. 430). This difference can be attributed to the depreciation charge of Rs. 300. The cash available with the firm is Rs. 430. This can be utilized for further investment. The accounting approach indicates that only Rs. 130 is available and-hence gives only a partial picture of the tangible benefits available. Clearly, such an approach does not bring out the total benefits of the project available for reinvesting. Therefore, in place of earnings, the cash flow information is employed in evaluating capital expenditure alternatives.

2. Cash Flow Pattern

Cash flow pattern can be classified as conventional or non-conventional

(a) Conventional Cash Flows: Initial cash outlay followed by series of cash in flows.

(b) Non-conventional Cash Flows: Alternating inflows and outflows and an inflow followed by outflows are examples of non-conventional cash flow patterns.

Year	0	1	2	3	4	5	Pattern of cash flow
Cash flows							
Case - 1	(1000)	500	1000	300	600	800	Conventional
Case -2	(1000)	500	1000	(700)	600	300	Non-conventional

3. Determination of Relevant Cashflows

The data requirement for capital budgeting are cash flows, that is, outflows and inflows. Their computation depends on the nature of the proposal. Capital projects can be categorized into :

(*i*) Single proposal

(*ii*) Replacement situations, and

(*iii*) Mutually exclusive.

(*i*) Single Proposal : The cash outflows comprising cash outlays required to carry out the proposed capital expenditure are depicted below:

Calculations of Cash Outflows ($t = 0$)

1. Cost of new project
2. + installation cost of plant and equipments.
3. ± Working capital requirements.

Calculation of cash Inflows ($t\pm \ldots n$)

1. Particulars	Years 1	2	3	4	N
Cash sales revenues					
Less : Cash operating cost					
Cash inflows before taxes (CFBT)					
Less : Depreciation					
Taxable income					
Less : Tax					
Earning after taxes					
Plus : Depreciation					
Cash inflows after tax (CFAT)					
Plus : Salvage value (in n^{th} year)					
Plus : Recovery of working capital (in i^{th} year)					

***(ii)* Replacement Situation :** In the case of replacement of an existing machine (asset) by a new one, the relevant cash outflows are after-tax incremental cash flows. If a new machine is intended to replace an existing machine, the proceeds so obtained from its sale reduce cash outflows required to purchase the new machine from a part of relevant cash flows. The calculation of after-tax incremental cash outflows is illustrated below :

(*i*) Cost of the new machine

(*ii*) + Installation cost

(*iii*) ± Working Capital

(*iv*) – Saie proceeds of existing machine

Depreciation Base in Case of Replacement Situation

(*i*) WDV of the existing machine.

(*ii*) + Cost of the acquisition of new machine (including installation costs).

(*iii*) – Sale proceeds of existing machine.

(*iii*) Mutually Exclusive Situations : In mutually exclusive proposals the selection of one proposal eliminates the choice of others. The calculation of Inflows and outflows is similar to replacement situation.

4. Cash Flow Estimation

Following points should be considered while estimating cash flows :

1. Cash flows to be considered should be net of taxes.
2. Cash flows effects of projects on other existing projects of the firm must be considered.
3. If the indirect expenses are affected as a result of investment decision, such amounts should be taken into account.

4. Depreciation, although a non-cash item of cost, is deductible expenditure in determining taxable income.
5. Working capital effect.

5. Working Capital Effect

Working Capital effect is an important ingredient of the cash flow stream which is directly related to an investment proposal.

The increased working capital forms part of the initial cash outlay. The additional net working capital will be returned to the firm at the end of the project's life. Therefore, the recovery of working capital becomes part of the cash inflow stream in the terminal year.

This increase in working capital should be considered as cash outflow of the year in which additional working capital is required.

All revenue expansion capital investment proposals require additional working capital, Likewise, almost all cost-reduction capital investment projects release the existing amount of working capital.

The effect of decrease in working capital white evaluating an investment project is the amount of working capital gets released should be seen as a cash inflow in the zero time period, reducing the net cash investment required for the project In the terminating year of the project, it should be treated as a cash outflow and adjusted against the cash inflow of that year.

6. Incremental Analysis

Incremental analysis is the widely prevalent practice. According to incremental analysis only differences due to the decision need to be considered. For the purpose of estimating relevant cash outflows and inflows in the analysis of investments, incremental case flows i.e., additional cash flows expected to result from a proposed capital expenditure are taken into account.

Relevant cash flow is the incremental after-tax cash outflow and resulting subsequent inflows associated with a proposal capital expenditure, in other words, incremental cash flows are adjusted for tax liability.

Investment Evaluation Techniques (or) Capital Budgeting Techniques

Three steps are involved in the evaluation of an investment:

- G Estimation of cash flows
- Q Estimation of the required rate of return
- Q Application of a decision rule for making the choice.

A number of capital budgeting techniques are in use in practice. They may be grouped in the following two categories:

1. Non-discounted cash flow criteria/traditional techniques.
   (*a*) Pay Back Period (PBP)
   (*b*) Accounting Rate of Return (ARR)
2. Discounted Cash Flow (DCF) Criteria/Modem Techniques
   (*a*) Discounted Pay Back Period (DPBP)
   (*b*) Net Present Value (NPV)
   (*c*) Internal Rate of Return (IRR)
   (*d*) Profitability Index (PI)

NON-DISCOUNTED CASH FLOW CRITERIA/ TRADITIONAL TECHNIQUES

(A) Pay Back Period (PBP): The payback period is the length of time required to recover the initial cash outlay on the project. For example, if a project Involves a cash outlay of Rs. 600,000 and generates cash inflows of Rs. 100,000, Rs. 150,000, Rs. 150,000 and Rs. 200,000, in the first, second, third, and fourth years, respectively, its payback period is 4 years because the sum of cash inflows during 4 years is equal to the initial outlay. When the annual cash inflows is a constant sum, the payback period is simply the initial outlay divided by the annual cash inflow. For example, a project which has an initial cash outlay of Rs. 1,000.000/300,000 = $3^1/_3$ years.

There are two ways of calculating the PB period.

(*i*) **Uniform Cash Flows:** The first method can be applied when the cash flow stream is in the nature of annuity for each year of the project's life, that is, CFAT are uniform. In such a situation, the initial cost of the investment is divided by the constant annual cash flow or uniform cash flows :

$$\text{PR} - \frac{\text{Investment}}{\text{Constant annual cashflow}}$$

(*ii*) **Non-uniform Cash Flows:** Payback is calculated by the process of cumulating cash flow till the time when cumulative cash flows become, equal to original investment.

In more simple words

PEP–Full years +

$$\frac{\text{Balance of the amount to be realised from investment}}{\text{cashflow of respective year}}$$

Balance amount * Investment – Total amount realized in full years.

Merits

1. It is simple in concept and application.
2. It is a rough and ready method for dealing with risk. It favours projects which generate substantial cash inflows in earlier years and discriminates against projects which bring substantial cash inflows in later years but not in earliest years. If risk tends to increase with future payback criterion may be helpful in weeding out risky projects.

Demerits

1. It ignores time value of money.
2. If ignores cash flows beyond the payback period. This leads to discrimination against projects which generate substantial cash flows in later years.
3. It is a measure of projects capita! recovery, not profitability.

Decision Rule

According to payback the shorter — the payback period the more desirable the project.

Pay Back Period (Non-Uniform Cash Flows):

Consider the cash flows of two projects A& B. Calculate PBP

Year	0	1	2	3	4	5	6
Cash flows							
A	(1,00,000)	50,000	30,000	20,000	10,000	10,000	–
B	(1,00,000)	20,000	20,000	20,000	50,000	50,000	60,000

Solution

	A		B	
Year	Cashflow	Cumulative Cash flows	Cash flows	Cumulative Cash flows
1	50,000	50,000	20,000	20,000
2	30,000	80,000	20,000	40,000
3	20,000	1,00,000	20,000	60,000
4	10,000	1,10,000	40,000	1,00,000
5	10,000	1,20,000	50,000	1,50,000
6			60,000	2,40000

Initial investment for both the projects is 1,00,000. Hence payback period for A = 3 yrs B = 4 yrs.

A Proposal Is expected to generate cash in flows of Rs. 8,000, 6,000, 4,000, 2,000 and Rs, 2,000 over next 5 years. Calculate PBP, of initial outlay required is —

(a) Rs. 20,000; *(b) 18,500.*

Solution

Year	Cashflow	Cumulative Cash flows
1	8,000	8,000
2	6,000	14,000
3	4,000	18,000
4	2,000	20,000
5	2,000	22,000

(*a*) PBP = 4 yrs

(*b*) $\text{PBP} = 3 \text{ yrs} + \dfrac{500}{2000} = 3.25 \text{ yrs.}$

The cumulative cash inflow is 18,000 at the end of 3 yrs. The outlay required is 18,500. Therefore cash inflow of 500 during 4th year would be sufficient to realize the investment. The precise period required to earn a cash Inflow of Rs. 500 during 4th year would be [500/2000 = 0.25] Hence payback period for an outflow of 18,500 is 3.25 years.

PBP (Uniform Cash Flows)

A proposal requires a cash outflow of Rs. 1,00,000 and is expected to generate cash inflows of 20,000 *P.A. for 6 years calculate PBP.*

Solution :

PBP for uniform cash flows =

$$\frac{\text{Investment } 1{,}00{,}000}{\text{Constant annual cashflow} = 20{,}000} = 5 \text{ years}$$

(B) Accounting Rate of Return (ARR)

Average rate of return is also known as accounting *rate of return*

$$ARR = \frac{\text{Average annual profits after taxes (PAT)}}{\text{Average investment over the rate of the project}}$$

$$\text{Average Investment} = \frac{\text{Book value of investment}}{2}$$

Case I : Non-uniform PAT

$$\text{Annual PAT} = \frac{\text{sum (PAT)}}{n}$$

Case II : Uniform PAT

Average PAT is equal to Annual PAT.

The average investment of the proposal over its economic life can also be calculated as follows when there is salvage value and working capital.

Average investment = 1/2 (Initial cost + installation expenses - salvage value) + salvage value + Additional working capital

In the above equation, the amount of salvage value has been first deducted and later added back. The.salvage value has been deducted to find out the annual amount of depreciation. However, this amount of salvage value remains blocked in the proposal and is released only at the end of the economic life of proposal. Therefore, the amount of salvage value has been added back to find out the average investment.

Similarly, the project may also require additional working capital for its smooth operations. Though this additional working capital will be released back, when the proposal will be scrapped and terminated. This amount of additional working capital is blocked through out the life of the project So, its additional working capital entails the investment of funds of the firm and should be added to be average investment calculated as above.

Merits

1. It is simple to calculate, understand and use.
2. It considers the benefits over the life of the project.

Demerits

1. It is based on accounting information and not cash flows.
2. It ignores time value of money.
3. The benefits in earlier and later years are taken at par and fails to take account of differences in time value of money.

Decision Rule

1. The higher the accounting rate of return, the better the project.
2. Discounted cash flow criteria / Modern techniques.

ARR (Non Uniform Profits)

Calculate rate of return for the following project.

Year	Book value of fixed investment	Prof it after tax
1	90,000	Rs. 20,000
2	80,000	22,000
3	70,000	24,000
4	60,000	26,000
5	50,000	28,000

Solution :

The accounting rate of return is :

$$\frac{1/5\,(20{,}000+22{,}000+24{,}000+26{,}000+28{,}000)}{1/5\,(90{,}000+80{,}000+70{,}000+60{,}000+50{,}000)} = 34 \text{ per cent}$$

The higher the accounting rate of return, the better the project.

ARR (Uniform Profits with Salvage Value a Working Capital)

ABC Ltd. consider the project costing 1,20,000 and with expected use of 5 years and salvage value of 20,000. 2 working capital of 20,000 and is expected to generate Avg. profit after taxes of Rs. 18,0001-. Calculate ARR.

Solution :

When there is salvage value and working capital

We know Average investment = – (initial cost + installation expenses – salvage value) + salvage value + additional working capital

Average Investment = 1/2 (1,20,000 – 20,000) + 20,000 + 20,000 = 90,000

ARR = PAT/ AVG INVESTMENT * 100 = 18000/90000* 100 = 20%

Example 6. *Determine average rate of return from the following data of two machines A – B*

Particular	Machine i	
	A	B
Cost	56,125	56,125
Annual estimated income after depreciation & income tax year		
Year 1	3,375	11,375
2	5,375	9.375
3	7,375	7,375
4	9,375	5,375
5	11,375	3,375
	36,875	36,875
Estimated Life	5 yrs	5 yrs
Estimated salvage value	3,000	3,000

Solution :

$$ARR - \frac{\text{Avg. annual profits after taxes (PAT)}}{\text{Average investment}}$$

AVG PAT = 36875/5 = 7375

Avg. investment = 1/2 (cost - salvage value) + Salvage value

= 1/2(56,125 – 3000) + 3,000 = 29,562.50

ARR (for both machines) = 7375/29562.5 = 24.9%

DISCOUNTED CASH FLOW (PCF) CRITERIA/ MODERN TECHNIQUES

(A) Discounted Payback Period (DPBP)

A major shortcoming of the conventional payback period is that it does not take into account the time value of money. To overcome this limitations, the discounted payback period has been suggested. In this modified method, cash flows are first converted into their present values (by applying suitable discounting factors) and then added to ascertain the period of time required to recover the initial outlay on the project.

Decision Rule

- According to payback the shorter-the payback period the more desirable the project.

From the following data calculate discounted PBP considering rate of 10%

Year	0	1	2	3	4	5	6	7
Cash flows	(10,000)	3,000	3,000	4,000	4,000	5,000	2,000	3,000

Solution :

	1	3	3 = 1x2	
Year	Cashflow	PV Factors® 10%	PVCF	Cumulative Cash flows
1	3,000	0.909	2,727	2,727
2	3,000	0.826	2,478	5,205
3	4,000	0.751	3,004	8,209
4	4,000	0.683	2,732	10,841
5	5,000	0.621	3.105	14,046
6	2,000	0.565	1,130	15,176
7	2,000	0.513	1,539	16,715

DPBP = 3 + 1791/2739 = 3 + 0.66 = 3.66 years

(B) Net Present Value

The net present value (NPV) of a project is the sum of the present values of all the cash flows — positive as well as negative — that are expected to occur over the life of the project. The general formula of NPV is :

$$SUM \{CFATt/(1+K)^t\} - Investment$$

$CFAT_t$ = Cash flow at the end of year t

n = Life of the project

k = discount rate Merits :

1. It recognizes time value of money and is based on cash flows.
2. It considers total benefits arising out of the proposal over the projects life.
3. NPV calculation permits time varying discount rates.
4. It is considered to be the best method in achieving the objective of financial management i.e., maximizations of shareholders wealth.

Demerits

1. It is difficult to calculate, understand and use in comparison with traditional methods.
2. It is an absolute measure.
3. It doesn't consider the life of the project's NPV rule is biased in favour of long-term projects.

Decision Rule

- The decision rule for a project under NPV is to accept the project if the NPV is positive and reject if it is negative. Symbolically,

  (*i*) NPV > Zero, accept (*ii*) NPV < zero, reject.
- Zero NPV implies that the firm is indifferent or rejecting the project.

NPV (Non-Uniform Cash Flows)—A Case of Conventional Project

Given the cash flows, calculate NPV of the project© 10% rate of return, with investment of Rs. 25,000 and cash inflows of 14,000, 16,000; 75,000 for 3 years.

Solution:

Initial investment is always at current period i.e., t_0 and indicate current outflow (C_0)

$$\text{NPV} = \frac{\text{present value of}}{\text{cash flows after taxes}} - \frac{\text{Present value of cash flows}}{\text{(initial investment)}}$$

$$\text{NPV of the project} = \sum_{t=1}^{n} \frac{CFAT_t}{(1+k)^t} - C_0$$

1 (1 + k)t is present value factor and

k represents rate of return i.e., 10%

$$\text{Present value} = \frac{1}{1+0.1} = \frac{1}{1.1 = 0.909;\ (1.1)\ (1.1)} = 0.826$$

Check A — 3 tables of respective rate and corresponding year for further values.

Calculation of NPV :

Year	CFAT	PV®10%	PVCFAT (CFDT × PV FACTOR)
0	(25,000)	1,000	(25,000)
1	14,000	0.909	12,726
2	16,000	0,826	13,216
3	18,000	0,751	13,518
	NPV	—	14,460

NPV (Uniform Cash Flows) : A Case of Non-Conventional Project

Given *Initial investment* - *25,000*

CFAT(t1-t3) - *15,000*

k - *10%*

Solution: Since the cash flows are uniform, we can consider the sum of present value factors and multiply with cash flow to get PVCFAT, The sum of present values are given in PV annuity tables {A – 4).

PVCFAT = 15,000 × PV annuity value @ 10% for 3 yrs.

= 15,000 (0.909 + 0.826 + 0.751);* – 15,000 × 2.486

NPV = SUM PVCFAT – C_0

NPV = 37,290 – 25,000 = 17,290

Example :

Year	CFAT	PV Factor® 10%	PVCFAT
0	(25,000)	1.000	(25,000)
1	14,000	0.909	12,726
2	(16,000)	0.826	(13,726)
3	(18,000)	0.751	13,518
4	20,000	0.683	13,660
	NPV		**14,904**

The above project involves an outflow in period to then inflow at t_1 and then outflow at t_2 and followed by inflow at t_3, t_4, Such project is called non-conventional project.

A project may be conventional or non-conventional, but the procedure for calculation of NPV is the same i.e., the sum of present value of outflows to be deducted from the sum of present value of inflows.

(C) Internal Rate of Return

The internal rate of return (IRR) of a project is the discount rate which makes its NPV equal to zero. It is the discount rate which equates the present value of future cash flows with the initial investment. It is the value of r in the following equation;

$$\text{Investment} = \sum_{t=1}^{n} \frac{CFAT_t}{(1+r)^t}$$

Where $CFAT_t$ = cash flow at the end of year

tr = internal rate of return (IRR)

n = life of the project

In the NPV calculation we assume that the discount rate (cost of capital) is known and determinate the NPV. In the IRR calculation, we set the NPV equal to zero and determine the discount rate that satisfies this condition.

The following is the procedure to estimate

1. Determine payback period (which is also called as fake pay back period)

   We know FPBP = $\dfrac{\text{Investment}}{\text{Avg. Annual cashflow}\left(\dfrac{\Sigma\text{Cashflows}}{\text{life of project}}\right)}$

2. Determine the net present value of the two closet rates of return.

   (NPV at 15 per cent) 802 in such a way that there is one +ve and one –ve NPV (NPV at 16 per cent) (1,359)

3. Find the sum of the absolute values of the net present values obtained in step 2 802 + 1359 = 2161

4. $\text{IRR} = \text{Lower rate} + \dfrac{\text{Desired NPV}}{\text{Total of NPV}} \times \text{Difference in rates}$

$$= 15 + \frac{802}{2161} * 1 = 15.37\%$$

Merits

1. IRR technique helps achieving the objective-of maximization of shareholders wealth.
2. IRR facilitates comparison with cutoff rates to analyze the proposals.
3. It considers cash flow, time value of money.

Demerits

1. It involves tedious, complicated trial and error methods.
2. It produces multiple rates which can be confusing.
3. It assumes that all the cash flows are reinvested at IRR which is considered unrealistic as it ignores timing of benefits.
4. In evaluating mutually exclusive proposals, the projects with highest IRR is closed which may not be in consistent with the objective of maximizing shareholders wealth.

Decision Rule

Accept: If the IRR is greater than the cost of capital

Reject: If the IRR is less than the cost of capital

IRR (Uniform Cash Flows)

A firm is evaluating a proposal costing Rs. 1,00,000 and having annual *inflows of Rs. 25,000 occurring at the end of each of next six years. There is no salvage value. The IRR of the proposal may be calculated as follows:*

Solution : Step 1 : The payback period in the given case is 4 years. The value nearest to 4 in the 6th year row of the PVAF table gives two closest rates i.e., 12% (4.111) and the rate 13% (3.998). This means that the IRR of the proposal is expected to lie between 12% and 13%.

Step 2 : In order to make a precise estimate of the IRR, find out the NPV of the project for both these rates as follows :

At 12%, NPV = (Rs. 25,000 × PVAF {12%, 6*y*) – Rs. 1,00,000

= (Rs. 25,000 × 4.111) – Rs. 1,00,000

= Rs. 2,775. At 13%, NPV = (Rs. 25,000 × PVAF(12%, 6y) – Rs. 1,00,000

= (Rs. 25,000 × 3.998) – Rs. 1,00,000

= Rs. –50

Step 3 : Sum of NPV's absolute values = 2,755 + 50 = 2825

Step 4 : IRR, = Lower rate + Desired NPV/Total NPV* *Difference in rates* 12 + 2775/2828 = 12.98%

Example 11. IRR (Non-uniform Cash Flows) : *A firm is evaluating a proposal costing Rs. 1,60,000 and expected to generate casr, inflows of Rs. 40,000, Rs. 60,000, Rs. 50,000, Rs. 50,000 and Rs. 40,000 at the end of each of next 5 years respectively. There is no salvage value thereafter. In this case, there is an uneven stream of cash inflows and the IRR can be approximated as follows :*

Step 1 : Calculate fake payback period using the following formula

$$\text{FBPB} = \frac{\text{Investment}}{\text{Average annual cashflows}}$$

Average annual cash flows = SUM (CASH FLOWS/LIFE OF THE PROJECT

= 40,000 + 60,000 + 50,000 + 50,000 + 40,000 / 5 = 48,000

= FBPB = 16000/48000

Step 2 : The value nearest to 3.288 in 5 years row of the PVAF table gives two closest figures at 15% (3.352) and at 16% (3.274). This means that the IRR of the proposal is expected to lie between 15% and 16%.

The NPV of the proposal for both of these approximate rates is as follows:

Year	Cash inflow	$PVF_{(16\times i5}y)$	$PVF_{(t5\%p5y)}$	PVF (16%)	PVF (16%)
1	40,000	0.862	0.870	34,480	34,480
2	60,000	0.743	0.756	44,580	45,360
3	50,000	0.641	0.658	32,050	32,900
4	50,000	0.552	0.572	27,600'	28,600
5	40,000	0.476	0.497	19,040	19,880
	Total			**1,57,750**	**1,61,540**

At 16%, NPV = Rs. 1,57,750 – Rs. 1,60,000 = –2,250 At 15% NPN = 1,61,540 – 1,60,000 = 1,540

Step 3: Sum of absolute values of NPV 1,540 + 2,250 = 3790 1540

Step 4: IRR = 15 + – j × 1

IRR = 15.40%

(D) Profitability Index (PI) or Benefit – Cost Ratio (B/C Ratio)

Another time-adjusted capital budgeting technique is profitability index (PI) or benefit-cost ratio (B/C). It is similar to the NPV approach. The profitability index approach measures the present value of returns per rupee invested, while the NPV is based on the different between the present value of future cash inflows and the. present value of cash outlays.

It is the ratio of present value of cash inflow and present value of cash outflows at a required rate of return.

$$\text{p/ (or) B/C ratio} = \frac{\text{Total present value of cash in flows}}{\text{Total present value of cash outflows}}$$

$$pI = \sum_{t=1}^{n} \frac{CFAT_t}{(1+k)^t} + C_0$$

This method is also known as the B/C ratio because the numerator measures benefits and the denominator costs. A more appropriate description would be present value index.

Decision Rule

- Using the B/C ratio or the PI, a project will qualify for acceptance if its PI exceeds one. When PI equals 1, the firm is. indifferent to the project.
- When PI is greater than, equal to or less than 1, the net present value is greater than, equal to or less than zero respectively. In other words, the NPV will be positive when the PI is greater than 1; will be negative when the PI is less than one. Thus, the NPV and PI approaches give the same results regarding the investment proposals. NPV is an absolute measure whfle it is a relative measure.

Example 12. *A firm is evaluating a proposal which requires a cash outlay of Rs. 40,000 at present and of Rs. 20,000 at the end of third from now. It is expected to generate cash inflows of Rs. 20,000, Rs. 40,000 and Rs. 20,000 at the end of 1st year 2nd year and 4th year respectively. Given the rate of discount of 10%*

Solution:

Year	Cash flows (Rs.)	$PVF_{(10X(n)}$	Present Values (Rs.)
0	–40,000	1,000	–40,000
1	20,000	0.909	18,180
2	40,000	0.826	33,040
3	–20,000	0,751	–15,020
4	20,000	0.683	13,660

Calculation of the Profitability Index

Present value of cash outflows

$$= \text{Rs. } 40{,}000 + 15{,}020 = 55{,}020.$$

Present value of cash inflows

= Rs. 18,180 + 33,040 + 13,660 = 64,880

$$\text{p/ (or) B/C ratio} = \frac{\text{Total present value of cash inflows}}{\text{Total present value of cash outflows}}$$

= 64880/55020 = 1.18

NPV. 1RR Is Methods—A Comparison

NPV and IRR.Similarities

The situations in which the two methods will give a similar accept-reject decision will be in respect of conventional and independent projects. A Conventional investment is one in which the cash flow pattern is such that an initial investment (outlay or cash outflow) is followed by a series of cash inflows. Thus, in the case of such investments, cash outflows are confined to the initial period. The independent proposals refer to investments the acceptance of which does not preclude the acceptance of others so that all profitable proposals can be accepted and there are no constraints in accepting all profitable projects. The projects which have positive net present values will also have an IRR higher than the required rate of return.

Incremental IRR

Incremental Analysis : Incremental analysis is the widely prevalent practice. According to incremental analysis, only differences due to the decision need to be considered. For the purpose of estimating relevant cash outflows and inflows in the analysis of investments, incremental cash flows i.e., additional cash flows expected to result from a proposed capital expenditure are taken into account.

Relevant cash flow is the incremental after-tax cash outflow and resulting subsequent inflows associated with a proposal capital expenditure, in other words, incremental cash flows are adjusted for tax liability.

Let us consider projects A & B involving cashflows as follows :

Cash Flows (Rs)				
Project	Co	Ci	NPV at 10%	IRR
A	–1,000	1,500	364	50%
B	–1,00,000	1,20,000	9,080	20%

Project A's NPV at 10 per cent required rate of return of Rs. 364 and IRR is 50 per cent. Project B's NPV at 10 per cent required rate of return is Rs. 9,080 and internal rate of return is 20 per cent. Thus, the two projects are ranked differently by the NPV and IRR rules.

Since the NPV of project B is high, it should be accepted. The same result will be obtained if we calculate the internal rate of return on the incremental investment:

Cash Flows (Rs)				
Project	Q.	Q	NPV at 10%	IRR
(A-B)	-99,000	118,500	8,716	19.7*

NPV and IRR Methods: Differences

In the case of independent conventional investments,, the NPV and IRR methods will give similar results. However, in certain situations they will give contradictory results such that if the NPV methods finds one proposal acceptable, IRR favours another.

The NPV and IRR rules will give conflicting ranking to the projects for the following reasons; (*i*) The cash flow pattern of the project is different (i.e.,) time disparity; (*ii*) The cash outlay of the project is different, (i.e.,) size disparity; (*iii*) The projects may have different expected lives (i.e.,) life disparity; (*iv*) Re-investment rate assumption; (*v*) Multiple IRR :

***(i)* Time Disparity:** Refers to a situation when larger cash inflows from one project may occur during early period of life time while for the other competitive proposal, at the end of economic life.

***(ii)* Size Disparity:** According to NPV, higher the cash inflows, larger would be the expected returns while IRR deals with returns in percentage form considering average cash inflows. For example if the data of inflows and outflows is doubled; NPV are also be double but, IRR remains unchanged and hence difference in ranking proposals.

***(iii)* Life Disparity:** In case of mutually exclusive projects or replacement decisions, it is assumed that life of the projects is equal. Though, the projects life is different it should not affect the choice of projects. But NPV and IRR give conflicting ranking to projects with unequal lives.

***(iv)* Reinvestment Rate Assumption:** NPV assumes that cash flows are reinvested at opportunity cost of capital while IRR assumes that cash flows are reinvested at IRR.

***(v)* Multiple IRR's:** In case of non-conventional investments there is problem of having multiple IRR's. This is a mathematical possibility that a complex proposal with varied cash inflows and outflows may result in two different IRR because of the pattern and timing of the inflows and outflows.

NPV Versus IRR: The IRR approach solves for a rate unique to each project, while the NPV approach solves for the trade-off cash inflows and outflows using a general required rate of return. On the basis of the above discussion of NPV and IRR, a comparison between the two may be attempted as follows :

(a) Superiority of IRR Over NPV: IRR may be considered superior to the NPV for the following reasons :

(i) IRR gives percentage return while the NPV gives absolute return.

(ii) For IRR, the availability of required rate of return is not a pre-requisite while the NPV it is must.

(b) Superiority of NPV Over IRR: The NPV is said to have superiority over IRR for

(*i*) NPV shows expected increase in the wealth of the shareholders.

(*ii*) NPV gives clear cut accept-reject decision rule, while the IRR may give multiple results also.

(*iii*) The NPV of different projects are additive while the FRRs cannot be added.

(*iv*) NPV gives better ranking as compared to the IRR.

(*v*) IRR rule cannot distinguish between lending and borrowing.

Of all the discounted cash flow techniques, NPV is considered superior for the reason that it maximizes the wealth of shareholders.

Conclusion Over DCF Techniques

The superiority of the discounted cash flow techniques over the traditional technique can be summarized as follow :

(*a*) The DCF techniques allows for the time value of money and are based on all the cash flows of the proposal.

(*b*) The DCF techniques are based on cash flows which are not affected by the discretionary accounting policies of the firm.

(*c*) In most of the cases, the DCF techniques provide a clear cut decision rule, and

(*d*) The risk associated with future uncertainties can be easily incorporated in the DCF techniques by adjusting the required rate of return or the cut-off rate.

ILLUSTRATIONS

Example 1. *A company is considering the replacement of its existing machine which is obsolete and unable to meet the rapidly rising demand for its product. The company is faced with two alternatives : (i) to buy machine A which is* *similar to the existing machine or (ii) to go in for machine B which is more expensive and has much greater capacity. The cash flows at the present level of operations under the two alternatives are as follows:*

Cash flows (in lacs of Rs.) at the end of year :

	0	1	2	3	4	5
Machine A	–25	—	5	20	14	14
Machine B	–40	10	14	16	17	15

The company's cost of capital is 10%. The finance manager tries to evaluate the machines by calculating the following :

1. *Net Present value;*
2. *Profitability index;*
3. *Payback period; and*
4. *Discounted payback.*

At the end of his calculations, however, the finance manager is unable to make up his mind as to which machine to recommended.

You are required to make these calculation and in the light thereof to advise the finance manager about the proposal investment.

Solution: NPV, PI, PBP, DPBP, Calculations are simplified by drafting all required calculations in a single table.

$$\text{pI (or) B/C ratio} = \frac{\text{Total present value of cash inflows}}{\text{Total present value of cash outflows}}$$

A = 37.35/25 = 1.494

B = 53.58/40 = 1.339

3. PBP in both the cases is 3 years in which the investment is fully realized.

4. DPBP:

A = 3 + 5.85(25-19.15)/ 9.52 = 3.614years

B = 3 + 7.28(40-32.72)/ 11.56 = 3.629 years

Year	Cash flows (CFAT)		Cumulative Cash flow for		PV factor 10% (A 3 tables)	PVCFAT CFATxPV		Cumulative PVCFAT for DPBP	
	A	B	A	B		A	B	A	B
0	(25)	(40)	(25)	(40)	1.000	(25)	(40)	(25)	(40)
1		10	—	10	0.91	—	9.10	—	9.10
2	5	14	5	24	0.83	4.15	11.62	4.15	20.72
3	20	16	25	40	0.75	15.00	12.00	19.15	32.72
4	14	17	39	57	0.68	9.52	11.56	28.67	44.28
5	14	15	53	72	0.62	8.68	9.30	37.35	53.58
1.					NPV	12.35	13.58		

Example 2. *The expected cashflows of a project are as follows:*

Year	0	1	2	3	4	5
Cash flows	(1,00,000)	20,000	30,000	40,000	50,000	30,000

The cost of capital is 12%. Calculate (i) DPBP and (ii) IRR. *(Nov. 2007)*

Solution: (*i*) DPBP

Year	CFAT	PV factor® 12%	PVCFAT	Cum. PVCFAT
1	20,000	0.893	17,860	17,860
2	30,000	0.797	23,910	41,770
3	40,000	0.712	28,480	70,250
4	50,000	0.636	31,800	1,02,050
5	30,000	0.567	17,010	1,19,060
	1,70,000			

DPBP = 3 + (1,00,000-70,250)/ 31800 = 3.93 yrs.

(*ii*) IRR :

Step 1 : FPBP = $\frac{\text{Investment}}{\text{Avg. Annual cashflows}} = \frac{1,00,000}{34,000} = 2.941$

Avg. annual cash flows = SUM (CASH FLOWS)/LIFE OF THE PROJECT

Step 2 : Locating above value in A-4 tables at 5th year the approximate rates between which the above values lies is 20% and 21%.

Year	CFAT	PV Factor 20%	PVCFAT	PVFAT® 18%	PVCFAT
0	(1,00,000)	1.000	(1,00,000)	1.000	(1,00,000)
1	20,000	0.833	16,660	0.847	16,940
2	30,000	0.694	20,820	0.718	21,540
3	40,000	0.579	23,160	0.609	24,360
4	50,000	0.482	24,100	0.516	25,800
5	30,000	0.402	12,060	0.437	13,110
			NPV	(3,200)	1,750

Step 3 : Sum of absolute values

3,200 + 1,750 = 4,950

Step 4 : IRR = 18 + 1750 / 4950 * 2 = 18 + 0.71 = 18.71%

Example 3. *A company is considering a capital investment proposal where 2 alternatives are being considered. Both investments have a 5 year life.*

In option 1 new machine would cost Rs. 2,78,000 and in option 2, Rs. 8,05,000. Anticipated scrap values after 5 years are Rs. 28,000 and Rs. 1,50,000 respectively.

Depreciation is provided on straight line basis option 1 would generate annual cash flows of Rs. 1,00,000 and option 2, Rs. 2,50,000. The cost of capital is 15%. Calculate for each option : (i) the pay back period (ii) The IRR (iii) The NPV, (iv) The IRR. *(Feb / March 2004)*

S.No.	Particulars	A	B
1.	Payback period		
	Investment Constant cash flow	2,78,000 1,00,000	8,05,000 2,50,000
		= 2.78	= 3.22
2.	ARR		•
	Average Annual PAT/ Average investment	50,000 / 1,53,000	1,19,000 / 4,77,000
		33%	25%
	WN CFAT	1,00,000	2,50,000
	Depreciation P.A	$\frac{2,78,000-28,000}{5}$ = 50,000	$\frac{8,05,000-1,50,000}{5}$ 1,31,000
PAT (CFAT - Depreciation)		50,000	1,19,000
Avg. investment 1/2 (cost-salvage value) + salvage value		1,53,000	4,77,000

3. NPV	Project A			Project B	
Year	CFAT	PV Annuity factor (915%	PVCFAT	CFAT	PVCFAT
1-5	1,00,000	3.352	3,35,200	2,50,000	8,38,000
5	salvage value 28,000	0.497	13.916	1,50,000	74,550
	Sum PVCFAT		3,49,116		9,12,550
	(–) Co		2,78,000		8,05,000
	NPV		71,116		1,07,550

4. IRR :

S.No.	Particulars	A	B
(*i*)	Fake payback period (Similar to PBP)	2.78	3.22
(*ii*)	Approximate rate of returns	23 & 24 %	16 a 17%
(*iii*)	NPV of project A		

Year	Parti-culars	Rs.	Present value	PV © 23% factor	PVCFAT	PV26%	PVCFAT
1-5	CFAT	1,00,000	Annuity	2.803	2,80,300	2.635	2,63,500
5	Salvage value	28,000	Factor	0.355	9,946	0.315	8,820
			PVCFAT	2,90,246			2,73,320
			(–)Co	2,78,000			2,78,000
	—		NPV ->	12,446			(5,680)

v The NPV is the +ve at 23% and we want a negative NPV, 26% is tried. (HI) Absolute sum of NPV's = 12,446 + 5,860 = 17,962

(*iv*) IRR of project A = 23 + 12,446 / 17296 * 3 = 23 + 2.05 = 25.05 %

(b) NPV of project B :

Year	Parti-culars	Rs.	Present value	PV © 17% factor	PVCFAT	PVR12%	PVCFAT
1-5	CFAT	2,80,000	Annuity	3,199	7,99,750	2.926	7,31,500
5	Salvage value	1,50,000	Factor	0.456	68,400	0.37	55,500
		£ PVCFAT	-»		8,68,150		7,87,000
		(–) Co	->		8,05,000		8,05,000
		NPV	->		63,150		(18,000)

v The NPV is the +ve at 17% and we want a negative NPV, 21% is tried. (Hi) Absolute sum of NPV's = 63,150 + 18,000 = 81,150

IRR =17+ 63150 / 81150 * 4 = 20.113%

Example 4. *A company is engaged in evaluating an investment project which requires an initix cash outlay of Rs. 2,50,000 on equipment. The project's economic life is 10 year, and its salvage value Rs. 30,000. It would require current assets of Rs. 50,000. Ar additional investment of Rs. 60,000 would also be necessary at the end of five years to restore the efficiency of the equipment. This would be written off completely over the last five years. The project is expected to yield annual profit (before tax) of Rs. 7,00,000. The company follows the sum of the year's method of depreciation. Income - tax rate is assumed to be 40%. Should the project be accepted if the minimum required rate of return is 20%.*

Solution: Calculation of Present values

Year	EBIT (Rs.)	DEP. (Rs.)	PBT (Rs.)	PAT (Rs.)® 60%	CFAT = PAT + DEP	Factor PV (15%)	PVCFAT (Rs.) (CFAT × PV factor
1	1,00,000	40,000	60,000	36,000	76,000	0.833	63,308
2	1,00,000	36,000	64,000	38,400	74,400	0.694	51,634
3	1,00,000	32,000	68,000	40,800	72,800	0.579	42,151
4	1,00,000	28,000	72,000	43,200	71,200	0.482	34,318
5	1,00,000	24,000	76,000	45,600	69,600	0.402	27,979
6	1,00,000	40,000	60,000	36,000	76,000	0.335	25,460
7	1,00,000	32,000	68,000	40,800	72,800	0.279	20,311
8	1,00,000	24,000	70,000	45,600	69,600	0.233	16,217
9	1,00,000	16,000	84,000	50,400	66,400	0.194	12,882
10	1,00,000	8,000	92,000	55,200	63,200	0.162	10,238
							3,04,498

PV of cash outflows (Rs.)		PV of Cash Inflows (Rs.)	
Initial cost	2,50,000	Annual Inttows($t_{.}$, . . . $_{10}$)	3,04,498
		Salvage value(t_{10}) 30,000	
Current assets	50,000	Current assets (t_{10}) 50,000	
Investment (Rs. 60,000 × $PVF_{,20\%}5_{y}$)	12,120	PVFX 80,000 i.e., 80,000 × 0.162	12,960
Total	**3,24,120**	**Total**	**3,17,458**
		(–) Co	3,24,120
		NPV	-> (6,662)

Since NPV is negative, Proposal should be rejected.
Working Notes :

1. The depreciation of different years have been calculated as per sum of the year's digit method as follows : Initial outlay—Salvage value i.e., Rs. 2,50,000 – Rs. 30,000 is to be depreciated over 10 years. The sum of the years digits for the years 1-10 is 55. So, depreciation for year 1 is 2,20,000 × (10/55) and for the year 2 it is 2,220,000' × (9.55) and so on. The total depreciation for first 5 years is Rs. 1,60,000 and so the written down value of the asset at the end of year *r*, is Rs. 90,000 (*i.e.*, Rs. 2,50,000 – 1,60,000). A capital expenditure of Rs. 60,000 is required at that stage. So, the total cost required to be depreciated is Rs. 1,20,000 (i.e., 90,000 + 60,000 - 30,000) and as per the year 6 is Rs. 1,20,000 × (5/15), for year 2 is Rs. 1,20,000 × (4.5) and so on.
2. The current assets of Rs. 50,000 would be released at the end of year 10 and therefore, it has been included in the inflow of year 10.

Example 5. *A Company is considering a new project for which the investment data are as follows:*

Capital Outlay	*Rs. 2,00,000*
Depreciation	*20% p.a.*

Forecasted annual income before charging depreciation, but after all other charges are as follows:

Year 1	*Rs. 1,00,000*
2	*1,00,000*
3	*80,000*
4	*80,000*
5	*40,000*
	4,00,000

On the basis of the available data, set out calculations, illustrating and comparing the following methods of evaluating the return :

(a) Payback method,

(b) Rate of return on original investment, and

(c) IRR.

Solution: Since there is no tax, the annual income before depreciation and after other charges is equivalent to cash flows (CFAT).

(*a*) Capital outlay of Rs. 2,00,000 is recovered in the first two years, (Rs. 1,00,000 (year 1) + Rs 1,00,000 (year 2), therefore, the payback period is the two years.

(*b*) Rate of return on original investment

Year	CFAT (Rs)	Depreciation (Rs)	Net Income (Rs)
1	1,00,000	40,000	60,000
2	1,00,000	40,000	60,000
3	80,000	40,000	40,000
4	80,000	40,000	40,000
5	40,000	40,000	2,00,000

Average income = Rs.200000/5 = Rs. 40,000

Rate of Return = Average income/Original investment × 100

40000/200000 × 100 = 20%

(*c*) Calculation of IRR :

Average CFAT.Total CFAT/No of Years = 4,00,000/5 = 80,000

Step 1 : FBPB : PB Value = Cash outflows/avg cfat = Rs. 2,00,000/ 80000 = 2.5 Years

Step - 2 : Factors closest to PB value of 2.5 corresponding to 5 years (life of the project) are 2.532 (28%) and 2.436 (30%). Since the actual cash flow stream is higher in initial years than average cash flows, higher discount rate of 33% may also be tried along with 30%.

Year	.CF(Rs)	PVFat 30 % 33%		Total PV (Rs.) 30 % 33%	
1	1,00,000	0.769	0.752	76,900	75,200
2	1,00,000	0.592	0.565	59,200	56,500
3	80,000	0.455	0.425	36,400	34,000
4	80,000	0.350	0.320	28,000	25,600
5	40,000	0.269	0.240	10,760	9,600
		PVCFAT		2,11,260	2,00,900
		(-) C_0		2,00,000	2,00,000
		NPV		11,260	900

As the NPV is +ve at 30% 33%. Let us try at 34%

Year	CF (Rs)	PV Factor ® 35%	PVCFAT
1	1,00,000	0.746	74,600
2	1,00,000	0.557	55,700
3.	80,000	0.416	33,280
4.	80,000	0.310	24,800
5	40,000	0.231	9240
	PVCFAT	1,97,620	
	(-) Co	*	2,00,000
	NPV	=>	(2,380)

Step 3 : Absolute sum of NPV's at 33% and 34% (two closest rates)

900 + 2,380 = 3,280

Step 4 : IRR = 33 + 900 /3280 * 1 = 33.38%

Example 6. *A Ltd whose required rate of return is 10% is considering to replace one of its plants by a new plant. The relevant data for the existing plant as well as the proposed plant are as follows :*

Evaluate the proposal as per both the NPV and the IRR techniques given that (i) the tax rate applicable to the firm is 40% and (ii) that the loss on disposal of an asset is not tax *deductible.*

	Existing Plant	**Proposed Plant**
Present book value /cost	24,000	54,000
Remaining life	6 years	6 years
Depreciation (per annum)	400	9,000
Salvage value (current)	20,000	
Profit before depreciation and		
tax (annual)	8,000	15,000

Solution: Incremental Net Investment or Net Initial Outflow :

Cost of the proposed plant	54,000
–Current scrap value of existing plant	20,000
Net cash outflow	34,000

Incremental annual cash inflows :

	Existing Plant	**Proposed Plant**
Profit before depreciation	8,000	15,000
–Depreciation	4,000	9,000
Profit before tax	4,000	6000
–Tax @ 40%	1,600	2,400
Profit after Tax	2,400	3,600
+Depreciation (added back)	4,000	9,000
Cash inflow	6,400	12,600

Therefore, incremental annual cash inflow 6,200

NPV of the proposal (required rate of return 10%) :

NPV = (Rs. 6,200 × $PVAF_{(10\%\ 6y)}$) – Rs. 34,000

= (Rs. 6,200 x 4.335) - Rs. 34,000 = Rs. -6,999 IRR:

$$1.\ \text{Fake payback period} = \frac{\text{Cash outflow}}{\text{Avg. annual cash flows}}$$

$$= \frac{34,000}{6,200} = 5.5 \text{ yrs.}$$

avg cash flow = sum (cash flows) / Life of the project = 6200/ 6 *6 = 6200

The payback period is 5.5 years. Now, on the basis of PVAF table, the values nearest to 5.5 in 6 years row are 5.601 (2%) and 5.242 (3%). Thus, the IRR of the proposal will lie between 2% and -3%, Since the cut-off rate is 10% which is much above than 3%, there is no purpose of calculation of the exact IRR.

The Decision : The proposal for replacing the old plant by a new one should be rejected. Both the NPV (i.e., Rs. –6,999) and the IRR (1.6., between 2% and 3% reject the proposal. Thus, the firm, may continue with existing plant only.

Example 7. *X Ltd. is considering the purchase of a new computer system for its Research and development division, which would cost Rs. 35 lacs. The operation and maintenance costs (excluding depreciation) are expected to be Rs. 7 lacs per annum, it is estimated that the useful life of the system would be 6 years, at the end of which the disposal value is expected to be Rs. 1 lac.*

The tangible benefits expected from the system in the form of reduction in design and draughtsmanship costs would be Rs. 12 lacs per annum. Besides, the disposal of used drawing office equipment and furniture, initially, is anticipated to net Rs. 9 lacs.

Capital expenditure in research and development would attract 100% write-off for tax purposes. The gains arising from disposal of used assets may be considered tax-free. The company's effective tax rate is 50%. The average cost of capital to the company is 12%, After appropriate analysis of cash flows, please advise the company of the financial viability of the proposal.

Solution:

1. Cash Outflow :	**Rs. In Lakhs**
Cost of new computer	35
– Disposal of Office	9
Net cash outflow	26

Particulars	Amt(Rs.)
Saving in design and draught draughtsmanship	12.00
(–) operation and maintenance cost	7.00
Gross Inflow	5.00
(–) Taxes @ 50%	2.50
Net Cash inflow P.A.	2.50

Year	Particulars	CFAT	PV@ 12%	PVCFAT
1	Tax savings on 35 lacs	17.50	0.893	15.628
1 -6	Cash Inflows	2.50	4.111	10.278
6	Salvage value	1.00	0.507	0.507
	PVCFAT			26,4125
	(–) Co			26.0000
	NPV			0.4125

As the NPV is positive Rs. 41,250, proposal may be accepted.

Example 8. *X Co. is considering a new automatic blender. The new blender would last for 10 years and would be depreciated to zero over the 10 year period. The old blender would also last for 10 more years and would be depreciated to zero over the same 10 , year period. The old blender has a book value of Rs. 20,000 but could be sold for Rs. 30,000 (the original cost was Rs. 40,000). The new blender would cost Rs. 1,00,000.*

It would reduce labour expense by Rs. 12,000 a year. The

company is subject to a 50% tax rate and the companys cost of capital is .8%.

Your are required to :

(I) Identify all the relevant cash flows for this replacement decision,

(ii) Compute the Net present value and profitability index.

(Hi) Find out whether this is an attractive project.

(CS, Final June 97)

Answer : 1. Calculation of Cash outflows :

Particulars	Amt(Rs.)
Cost of new machine	1,00,000
(–) Sale value of old machine	30,000
	70,000
(+) Additional tax due to profit on sale of old machine (10,000 × 50%) Profit = Sale Value - Book value = 30,000-20,000 = 10,000	5,000
Net Cash outflow	75,000.

2. Calculation of Cash Inflows

Cost savings in labour expenses	12,000
(–) Additional cost due to Increase in depreciation	
New depreciation = 1,00,000 /10 = 10,000	
(–) Old depreciation = 20,000 / 10 = 2,000	8.000
Increased earnings before taxes (EBT)	4,000
(–) taxes @ 50* i.e., (4000 × 50%)	2.000
Earnings after taxes (EAT)	2,000
(+) Depreciation	8,000
Increased after-tax annual cash flow	10,000

Calculation of NPV :

Year	CFAT	PV Annuity value @ 8%	PVCFAT
1 -10	10,000	6.71	67,100
(–)	Co		75,000 (7900)

The NPV is negative, the project is not attractive

Example 9. *A machine purchased four years.ago has been depreciated to its current book value of Rs. 50,000. The machine originally had a projected life of 10 years and zero salvage value.*

A new machine will cost Rs. 80,000. Its installation cost estimated by the technician is Rs. 20,000. The technician also estimates that the installation of the new machine will result in a reduced operating cost of Rs. 30,000 per year for the next 6 years. The old machine would be sold for Rs. 20,000. The new machine will have a 6-year life with no salvage value. The company's income is taxed at 35 per cent. Assuming the cost of capital at 12 per cent, determine whether the existing machine should be replaced. Make your own assumption regarding depreciation of the machine.

(Jan. 2007)

Solution:

Working Notes :

1. Calculation of profit or loss on sale of old machine :

Particulars	Amt (Rs.)
Book value of machine	50,000
(–) sale value	20,000
Loss on sale	30,000

2. Calculation of Depreciation Cost

Particulars	Amt (Rs.)
Depreciation on new machine = 80,000 + 20,000 / 6	16,667
Old Machine = 50,000 / 6	8,333
(Under the assumption that old machine would be depreciated to zero over the remaining life of 6 years)	
Additional depreciation cost on purchase of new machine	8,333

3. Calculation of Cash Outflows :

Particulars	Amt(Rs.)
Cost of new machine	80,000
Add installation charges	20,000 1,00,000
(–) Sale value of old machine	20,000 80,000
(–) Tax saving due to loss on sale of old machine (30,000 × 35%)	10,500
Net cash outflow (Co)	69,500

4. Calculation of cash inflows

Particulars	Amt (Rs.)
Saving in operating costs	30,000
(–) additional cost of depreciation PUT {-) Taxes ® 35% PAT	21,667 8,333 7,583 14,084
(+) Depreciation	-8,333
Increased CFAT P.A.	22,417

Calculation of NPV

Year	CFAT	PVAF® 12%	PVCFAT
1 -6	22,417	4.111	92,156
(–)	Co		69,500
	NPV		22,656

Since the NPV of the project is positive, it is suggested to replace the existing machine with new machine.

Example 10. *A company is considering the purchase of a machine to produce a new product. The new product will generate revenues of Rs. 60,000 per year for 5 years. The cost of materials and labour needed to generate these revenues will total Rs, 35,000 per year and other cash expenses will be Rs. 3,000 per year, net working capital of Rs. 4,500 will* *be required immediately and this amount will be freed up at the end of the fifth year. The machine will cost Rs. 30,000. It will be depreciated on a straight line basis over its five year life. The tax rate is 40% and the cost of capital is 12 % using the net present value, determine whether the machine has to purchased or not.* ***(Sept. 2003)***

Solution: Calculation of Cash outflows

Particulars	**Amt (Rs.)**
Cost of new machine	30,000
(+) Additional working capital	4,500
Net cash outflow	34,500

Calculation of Cash Inflows

Particulars	Amt (Rs.)
Revenue	60,000
(–) Cost of material, labour & cash expenses	38,000
Gross revenue	22,000
(–) Depreciation(60000/5)	12,000
PBT	10,000
(–) Taxes ® 40%	4,000
PAT .	6,000
(+) Depreciation cash flow after taxes	12,000 18,000
(+) Release of working capital	4,500
$CFAT_5$	22,500

Calculation of NPV

Year	CFAT	Present value ® 1 2%	PVCFAT
1-4	18,000	Annuity (A-4) 3.037	34, 672
5	22,500	Factor (A-3) 0.567	12,767
		PVCFAT	67,439
		(–) Co	34,500
		NPV	32,939

The NPV is +ve, the machine should be purchased.

Capital Budgeting, Risk and Uncertainty

Introduction : Risk analysis should be incorporated in the capital budgeting exercise. In general, other things being equal, a firm would be advised to accept a project which is less risky and reject those that involve more risk with the assumption that the management is averse to risk.

The capital budgeting decision is based on the benefits derived from the project. These benefits are measured in terms of cash flows. These cash flows are estimates and the actual returns will vary from the estimate. This is technically referred to as risk.

Definition : The risk with reference to capital budgeting/ investment decision many, therefore, be defined as the variability in the actual returns emanating from a project over its working life, in relation to the estimated return as forecast at the time of the initial capital budgeting decision.

Assumptions of Capital Budgeting Under Risk

The discussion on capital budgeting under risky situations is based upon the following assumptions :

(*i*) That the firm is not having any capital rationing, and no profitable project will be rejected for want of funds.

(*ii*) That the proposal's net investment is known with certainty.

(*iii*) Each set of cash flows is known with certainty.

(*iv*) The required rate of return of the firm reflects risk-return characteristics of the proposal.

(*v*) The firm is considered to be risk averse in the sense proposal with higher return is preferred among proposals with same risk and proposal with lower risk is preferred among proposals with same return.

UNCERTAINTY RISK and CERTAINIY

The decision situations with reference to risk analysis in capital budgeting decisions can be broken up into three types :

(*i*) Uncertainty, (*ii*) Risk and (*iii*) Certainty

The risk situation is one in which the probabilities of occurrence of a particular event are known. These probabilities are not known under the uncertainty situation. The difference between risk and uncertainty, therefore, lies in the fact that variability is less in risk than in uncertainty. In other words, in mathematical sense, risk reflects a set of unique outcomes for a given event for which probabilities can be assigned implying that the decision maker has some historical data on the basis of which probabilities are assigned to projects.

While uncertainty refers to a set of unique outcomes for a given element, for which probabilities cannot be assigned as the decision makers has no historical information and must make intelligent guesses in order to develop a subjective probabilities distribution.

In brief risk, with reference to capital budgeting refers to "the *variation between the estimated and actual returns*". The greater, the variability between estimated and actual, the more risky is the project.

Types of Risks

Risk is composed of demands that bring in variations in return of income and is influenced by external and internal considerations and thus can be classified into two types :

1. Systematic Risk : This risk is also called as external risk and are controllable. Hence it is a non-diversifiable risk. It is associated with securities market as well as the economic, sociological, political, psychological and legal considerations if the prices of all securities in the economy and hence cannot be avoided. The market portfolio represents the limit to attainable diversification because individual investors cannot hold a more diversified portfolio than the market portfolio.

Thus risk associated with market portfolio is systamatic (unavoidable) and is therefore non-diversifiable risk. Market risk, interest rate risk and purchasing power risk are grouped under systematic risk.

2. Unsystematic Risk : This risk is unique to a firm or industry. It is caused by factors like labour strike, irregular avoidable as it is caused by internal factors. It consists of :

(*a*) Business Risk, and

(*b*) Financial Risk

(a) Business Risk : business risk is that portion of the unsystematic risk caused by the operating environment of the business. Business risk arises from the inability of affirm to maintain its competitive edge and the growth or stability of the earnings. Variation that occurs in the operating environment is reflected on the operating income and expected dividends. The variation in the expected operating income indicates the business risk.

(b) Financial Risk : Financial risk in a company is associated with the capital structure of the company. It refers to the variability of the income to the equity capital due to the debt capital. The debt financing increases the variability of the return to the common stock holders and affects their expectations regarding the return.

Risk in Capital Budgeting Analysis

Several techniques are available to handle the risk perception of capital budgeting proposals. The technique which we deal grouped as follows.

I. Conventional *Techniques* :

(a) Risk adjusted discount rate (RADR)

(b) Certainty equivalent (GE)

(c) Sensitivity analysis.

II. *Statistical Technique?* :

(a) Probability distribution approach

(b) Decision free approach.

I. CONVENTIONAL TECHNIQUES

(a) Risk Adjusted Discount Rate (RADR)

The more uncertain returns in the future, the greater the risk and the greater the premium required. Based on this reasoning, it is proposed that the risk premium be incorporated into the capital budgeting analysis through the discount rate. That is, if the time preference for money is to be recognized by discounting estimated future cash flows, at some risk-free rate, to their present value, then, to allow for the riskiness, of those future cash flows a risk premium rate may be added to risk-free discount rate. Such a composite discount rate, called the *risk-adjusted* discount rate, will allow for both time preference and risk preference and will be a sum of the *risk-free* rate and *risk-premium* rate reflecting the investor's attitude towards. The risk-adjusted discount rate method can *be* formally expressed as follows :

$$NPV = \sum_{t=1}^{n} \frac{NCF_t}{(1+k)^t} - C_0$$

RADR assumes that investors are risk averse and demand premium for assuming risk Where k is a risk-adjusted rate.

Risk adjusted discount rate *(k)* = Risk free rate + risk premium for additional risk. $k = R_f + R_m$ CAPM and Concept of B : Capital asset pricing model (CPAM) provides a framework for basic risk return trade off portfolio management. It enables to asses risk and the size of risk premium necessary to compensate additional risk. CAPM links systematic risk and returns of all assets/securities. Thus, the measure/index of systematic risk is beta coefficient (p). Beta measures the sensitivity of returns of a security to changes in returns on the market portfolio. High p indicates greater r.

The beta of a security is computed according to the following equation

$$R_j = R_f + b_j R_p + e_j$$

Where *R$* = the required / expected return on asset, *j*

QJ = the intercept that equals the risk free rate, /?/.

Cj = random error term, which reflects the diversifiable risk of asset,*j*

ty = the beta coefficient which equals

$$\beta = \frac{COV(R_j, R_P)}{\sigma_P^2}$$

Where

COV *(Rj, R_p)* = Covariance of the return on asset;, j, and market portfolio, R_p. It is equal to

$$\sum_{t=1}^{n}(R_{jt} - R_j)(R_{pt} - R_P)(n-1)$$

sdp^2 = Variance of the return on the market portfolio

R_p = Required rate of return on the market of securities.

Equation Given beta as the index of relevant (systematic) risk, the CAPM is given as:

$$R_J = R_f + \beta_J \times (R_P - R_f)$$

Where *Rj* = the required rate of return on asset, *j*

Rf = the rate of return on a risk-free asset *Pj* = the beta coefficient of systematic (relevant) risk for asset *j*.

Rp = The required rate of return on the market portfolio of assets, that is, the average rate of return on all assets.

Advantages *of RADR*

1. It is simple and can be easily understood.
2. It is profit oriented and consider time value of money.
3. It is appealing to risk averse businessman as it incorporates attitudes towards uncertainty.

Limitations of RADR

1. It is difficult to derive risk-adjusted rate for it is based on other parameters like risk premium; *p*.

2. It doesn't make any risk adjustment to future cash flows. Which are risky and uncertain and is overcome by probability distribution approach.

RADR is always higher than the original discount rate i.e., k. The RADR reflect the return that must be earned by a proposal to compensate the firm for undertaking the risk. The higher the risk of a proposal, the higher the RADR would be and therefore the lower the NPV of a given set of cash flows.

Decision Rule : Accept the proposal if the RANPV is positive or even zero and reject the proposal if it is negative. In case of mutually exclusive proposals, the rule may be : select the alternative which has the highest positive RANPV.

In case, the firm is applying the IRR technique for evaluation of capital budgeting proposals, then the IRR of the project can be compared with the RADR i.e., the minimum required rate of return to accept or reject the proposals.

Example 1. *A project requires an investment of Rs. 11,11,111 & is expected to generate cash inflows of Rs. 3,33,333,. Rs. 4,44,444, Rs. 5,55,555, Rs. 4,44,444 and Rs. 3,33,333 for the next 5 years. The risk free cost of capital is 11%. Evaluate the project using IRR method if a risk premium of 9% is considered, how do you evaluate the project and do you observe any change in your earlier decision ?*

(Jan. 2005)

Solution:

$$\text{1.Fake payback period} = \frac{\text{Investment}}{\text{Average Annual cashflow}}$$

$$\text{Average Annual Cashflow} = \frac{\Sigma\text{Cashflows}}{\text{Life of the project}}$$

$$= 21,11,109/5 = 4,22,221$$

FBPB = 11,11,111/ 4,22,221 = 2.632

2. The above value lies appx between 26% and 27% at 5 years

3. Calculate of NPV's.

Year	CFAT	PV Factor 26%	PVCFAT	PV Factor 27%	PVCFAT	PV Factor 25%	PVCFAT
0	(11,11,111)	1.000	(11,11,111)	1.000	(11,11,111)	1.000	(11,11,111)
1	3,33,333	0.794	2,64,666	0.787 -	2,62,333	0.8	2,66,666
2	4,44,444	0.630	2,80,000	0.620	2,75,555	0.64	2,84,444
3	5,55,555	0.500	2,77,778	0.488	2,71,111	0.512	2,84,444
4	4,44,444	0.397	1,76,444	0.384	1,70,666	0.410	1,82,222
5	3,33,333	0.315	1,05,000	0.303	1,05,000	0.328	1,09,333
		NPV	7,223		26,445		15,998

Since the NPV is –ve at 26% and we want a +ve NPV lets try at 25%.

4. IRR = 25 + 15,998 / 23221 * 1 = 25.6 %

Decision : As IRR > Rf, 25.69 > 10% - accept; Also 25.68 > 19% – accept the project

The project can be accepted as it is more than the sum of risk free and risk premium *rates. The earlier decision does not change even of risk premium is considered.*

(b) Certainty Equivalents (CE):

An alternative approach to incorporate the risk is to adjust the cash flows of a proposal to reflect the riskiness. The CE approach attempts at adjusting the future cash flows instead of adjusting the discount rates. The expected future cash flows which are taken as risky and uncertain are converted into certainty cash flows. The extent of adjustment will vary and it can be either subjective or based on a risk return model. These adjusted cash flows are then discounted at risk free discount rate to findout the NPV of the proposal.

Procedure for CE approach can be explained as follows :

1. Estimation of future cash flows from the proposal (CFAT).
2. The a CE factors represents the level of present money at which the firm would be indifferent between accepting the present money or the future cash flow. For example, cash inflow of Rs. 10,000 is receivable after 2 years.

However, if the inflow is available right now, the firm may be ready to accept even 70% of Rs. 10,000 i.e., Rs. 7,000 only, This 70% or .7 is the CE factor.

3. Certainty cash flows (a CF)
4. Find out present value of certainty cash flows at risk free rate (K).

$$PVCCF = \sum_{t=1}^{n} \frac{\alpha_t CF_t}{(1+k)} - C_0$$

5. Calculate Risk adjusted NPV (RANPV) : Step 4 - Initial investment.

CE factors (a) will vary between 0 and 1 and will vary inversely to risk. The greater the risk involved, the lower will be the CE factor (a) can be determined arbitrarily using the following ratio.

$$\alpha = \frac{\text{Certainty cash flows}}{\text{Expected cash flows}}$$

Advantages

1. The CE approach recognizes risk and incorporates reducing cash flows to CE cash flows.
2. CE approach is conceptually superior to RABR as it does not assume that risk overtime at a constant rate.

Limitation

Determination of CE factor is a tedious Job. Decision Rule :

+ve CE NPV = Accept -veCENPV = Reject

If a firm is using IRR technique to evaluate the capital budgeting proposals, then the IRR of the CE cash flows can be calculated and compared with the minimum required rate of return to make an appropriate decision.

RADR, CE — A Comparison

S.No.	RADR	CE
1.	It incorporate risk by increasing the discount rate	it Incorporates risk by reducing the expected cash flows.
2.	It deals with denominator of NPV.	It deals with numerator of NPV.
3.	Assumes that risk of the proposal increases at a constant rate over life of project	Incorporates different degrees of risk involved for different years.
4.	Considers risk, risk free rate and risk premium together.	Maintains distinction between risk rate and risk.
5.	Single adjustment for risk and time	Separate adjustment for risk and time

Example 1. *ABC and Co. is considering two mutually exclusive machines X and Y. The company uses a certainty equivalent approach to evaluate the proposals. The estimated cash flow and certainty equivalents for both machines are as follows :*

	Machine X		Machine Y	
Cash flow	Cer. Eqult. Rs.	Year	Cash flow Rs.	Cer. Eqult.
0	–3 0,000	1.00	–40,000	1. 00
1	75,000	0.95	25,000	0.90
2	75,000	0.35	20,000	0.80
3	70,000	0.70	75,000	0.70
4	70,000	0.65	70,000	0.60

Which — machine should be accepted, if the risk free discount rate is 5 per cent.

Solution :

Project - A						Project B			
Year	CFAT	CE(a)	CECFAT	PV@ 5%	PV (CEC FAT) 5%	CFAT	CE(a)	CECFAT	PV (CEF CAT)@ 5%
0	(30,000)	1.00	(30,000)	1.000	(30,000)	(40,000)	1.00	(40,000)	(40,000)
1	15,000	0.95	14.250	0.952	13,566	25,000	0.90	22,500	21,420
2	15,000	0.85	12,750	0.907	11,564	20,000	0.80	16,000	14,512
3	10,000	0.70	7,000	0.864	6,048	15,000	0.70	10,500	9,072
4	10,000	0.65	6,500	0.823	5,350	10,000	0.60	6,000	4,938
	Risk adjusted NPV (RANPV)				6,528				9,942

CECFAT = CFAT x CE

PVCECFAT = CECFAT x PV factor.

Decision : Machine Y should be accepted as its RANPV is higher than machine X.

Example 2. *A project requires an investment of Rs. 1,44,000 and is expected to generate cash in flows of Rs. 54,000, Rs. 63,000, Rs. 72,000, Rs. 63,000 and Rs. 54,000 P.A. For the next 5 years. The risk free rate is 10%. Evaluate the project using IRR method. If the following certainty equivalents are to be considered, how would you evaluate and interpret the project.* *(Sept. 2004)*

Year	1	2	3	4	5
CF	0.96	0.92	0.88	0.82	0.79

1.Calculation of CENPV :

Year	CFAT Cash Flow	CE_2	CECFAT	PV factor @ 10%	PVCECFAT
0	(1,44,000)	1.00	(1,44,000)	1.000	(1,44,000)
1	54,000	0.96	51,840	0.909	47,123
2	63,000	0.92	57,960	0.826	47,875
3	72,000	0.88	63,360	0.751	47,583
4	63,000	0.82	51,660	0.683	35,284
5	54,000	0.79	42,660	0.621	26,492
			RANPV		60,357

The risk adjusted NPV is positive, accept the project.

2. Calculation of IRR :

(*i*) Fake payback period = Investment/ Avg annual cash flow = 144000/61200 = 2.353

(*ii*) 2.353, the above value lies appx between 31% and 32% at 5 years,

(*iii*) Calculation of NPV

Year	CFAT	PV Factor ® 32%	PVCFAT	PV factor ® 32%	PVCFAT
0	(1,44,000)	1.000	(1,44,000)	1.000	(1,44,000)
1	54,000.	0.763	41,202	0.758	40,932
2	63,000	0.583	36,729	0.574	36,162
3	72,000	0.445	32,040	0.435	31,320
4	63,000	0.340	21,420	0.329	20,727
5.	54,000	0.259	13,986	0.250	13,500
		NPV	1,377		1,359,

4. IRR = 31 + 1377 / 2736 * 1 = 31.5 %

Conclusion

ARR = $\frac{2,04,357/5}{144000/5} = \frac{40,871}{72000}$ = 58%

The average rate of return from project on the basis of PVCECFAT and Average investment is 57% which is higher than IRR. Hence the project is acceptable on the basis of IRR and CE methods.

(c) Sensitivity Analysis : One measure which expresses risk in more precise terms is sensitivity analysis. It provides information as to how sensitive the estimated project parameters, namely, the expected cash flow, the discount rate and the project life are to estimation errors. The analysis on these lines is important as the future is always uncertain and there will always be estimation errors. Sensitivity analysis takes care of estimation errors by using a number of possible outcomes in evaluating a project The method adopted under sensitivity analysis is to evaluate a project using a number of estimated cash flows to provide to the decision maker an insight into the variability of the outcomes.

Sensitivity analysis provides different cash flow estimates under

(*i*) the worst (i.e., the most pessimistic),

(*ii*) The expected (i.e. the most likely),

(*iii*) The best {i.e., the most optimistic) outcomes associated with the project.

Limitations

1. It is neither a risk measuring nor a risk reducing technique.
2. It doesn't provide any clear out decision, rule i.e. It doesn't provide any sense of likelihood of occurring of values.
3. Sensitive analysis is subjective analysis, i.e., one decision maker may reject the proposal while other may accept it. .

Despite the above limitations, sensitive analysis provides the decision maker with more than one estimate of the projects outcome and variability of returns.

II. STATISTICAL TECHNIQUES

(a) Probability Distribution Approach

It has been shown above that sensitivity analysis provides more than one estimate of the future return of a project. It is, therefore, superior, as it gives a more precise idea regarding the variability of the returns. But it has a limitation in that it does not disclose the chances of occurrence of these variations. To remedy this shortcoming of sensitivity analysis so as to provide a more accurate forecast, the probability of the occurring variations should also be given. Probability assignment to expected cash flow, therefore, would provide a more precise measure of the variability of cashflows. The concept of probability is helpful as it indicates the percentage change of occurrence of each possible cash flow.

The probability of obtaining particular cash flow estimates would be between 0 and 1.

The quantification variability of returns *involve two steps*

1. Assigning of probabilities.
2. Estimation of expected return of the projects in terms of expected monetary values (EMV) or is given as expected value of cash flows {EVCF).

EVCF (or) EMV mean = Cash flows x Probability

$$NPV = \sum_{t=1}^{n} \frac{EMV}{(1+k)^t} - C_0$$

Decision Rule : The project with higher return is preferred.

The assignment of probabilities and the calculation of EMV's takes into account risk in terms of variability. But it does not indicate the extent of variability, hence arising the need for a precise statistical measure.

Precise Measures of Risk : Standard Deviation and Coefficient of Variation:

Standard deviation (a) and the coefficient of variation

(CV) are two such measures which tell us about the variability associate with the expected cash flow in terms of degree of risk. Standard deviation is an absolute measure which can be applied when the projects involve the same outlay. If the projects to be compared involve different outlays, the coefficient of variation is the correct choice, being a relative measure.

***(i)* Standard Deviation :** Absolute Measure of Risk : SD is a measure that indicates the degree of uncertainty of cash flows. In statistical terms, standard deviation is defined as the square root of the mean of the squared deviation, where deviation is the difference between an outcome and the expected mean value of all outcomes.

$$\text{Mean} = \overline{CF} = EMV$$

$$\sigma = \sqrt{P_1(CF_1 - \overline{CH})^2 + P_2(CF_2 - \overline{CF})^2 + ...P_n(CF_n - \overline{CF})^2}$$

$$\sigma = \sqrt{\sum_{t=1}^{n} P_1(CF_1 - \overline{CF})^2}$$

The greater the standard deviation of a probability distribution, the greater is the risk.

If two projects have the same expected value (mean), then one which has a greater <y will be said to have higher degree of uncertainty or risk.

Hence, the project with lesser standard deviation is preferred as it has low risk.

(11) Coefficient of Variation (CV), A relative measure of risk : On the basis of risk and return, projects with high return and low risk are preferred. In case where one project has high risk and high return and other has low risk and low return, it is difficult to make a decision on the basis of *a*. Coeff. of variation resolves this dialema.

$$CV = \frac{\sigma}{EMV}$$ Lesser CV less risky is the project

Higher CV high risky is the project Decision Rule : Project with lesser CV is preferred.

EXAMPLES

Example 1. *Project A and B require an investment of Rs. 20,00,000 each, the life of both the projects is five* years. *The Information about projected cash inflows and probabilities is given below:* ***(July 2005)***

	Project "A" RS.	Probability	Project "B* Rs.	Probability
Optimistic	8,00,000	0.4	10,00,000	0.2
Moderate	7,00,000	0.2	9,00,000	0.1
Poor	6,00,000	0.3	7,00,000	0.4
Pessimistic	5,00,000	0.1	6,00,000	0.3
		1.0		1.0

You are required to calculate NPV and rank the projects. The cost of capital of the company is 10% of P.A.

Solution :

	Project A			Project B		
Condition	CFAT	Prob	EMV	CFAT	Prob	EMV
Optimistic	8,00,000	0.4	3,20,000	10,00,000	0.2	2,.00,000
Moderate	7,00,000	0.2	1,40,000	9,00,000	0.1	90,000
Poor	6,00,000	0.3	1,80,000	7,00,000	0.4	2,80,000
Pessimistic	5,00,000	0.1	50,000	6,00,000	0.3	1,80,000
1	EMV		6,90,000			7,50,000
2 - 5 years	PV annuity value 10%		3.791			3.791
3	PVEV (1x2)		26,15,643			28,43,250
4	Co		20,00,000			20,00,000
5	NPV (3-4)		6,15,643			8,43,250
6	Ranking		I			I

As the NPV of project B Is more than A, project B is preferable

***Example 2.** ABC and Co. is evaluating a proposal having initial outlay* of Rs. *1,40,000 and economic life of 2 years. The cash inflows and the respective probabilities have been found to be as follows* :

Year 1		Year 2	
Cash inflows Rs.	**Prob.**	**Cash inflows Rs.**	**Prob**
1,00,000	0.3	1,40,000	0.5
80,000	0.5	70,000	0.3
10,000	0.2	60,000	0.2

Evaluate the *proposals given that the firm has minimum required rate of return of 10%.*

Solution : Step 1 : *Calculation of EMV of cash inflows*

Year 1			Year -2		
Inflows	**Prob.**	**Prob EMV×Inflows**	**Inflows**	**Prob.**	**Prob EMVxInflows**
1,00,000	0.3	30,000	1,40,000	0.5	70,000
80,000	0.5	40,000	70,000	0.3	21,000
10,000	0.2	2,000	60,000	0.2	12,000
EMV		72,000			1,03,000

Step 2 : Calculation *of NPV of the* Proposal-

EMV	**Year (n)**	**$PVF_{(10x,n)}$**	**PVEMV**
–1,40,000	0	1.000	–1,40,000
72,000	1	0.909	65,448
1,03,000	2	0.826	85,078
NPV =			10,526

The proposal therefore, is expected to have a NPV of Rs. 10,526 and may be accepted.

Example 3. The *following data in respect of a proposal having an outlay of Rs. 6,000 has been submitted before PQR and Co.*

Year	Inflows	Prob.	Year	Inflows	Prob.
1	1,00	0.1	3	1,500	0.1
	1,500	0.2		2,200	0.1
	2,000	0.4		2,800	0.7
	2,500	0.2		3,500	0.1
	3,000	0.1			
2.	2,000	0.2			
	2,500	0.3			
	2,700	0.2			
	2,800	0.3			

Evaluate the proposal given that the discount rate is 15%.

Solution :

The calculation of the NPV of the proposal can be made as follows :

Year	CFAT	Prob.	EMV=Prob x CFAT	ΣEMV	$PVF_{05\%,n)}$	PV EMV
0	-6,000	1.0	-6,000	-6,000	1.000	-6,000
1	1,000	0.1	100			
	1,500	0.2	300			
	2,000	0.4	800			
	2,500	0.2	500			
	3,000	0.1	300	2,000	0.870	1,740
2.	2,000	0.2	400			
	2,500	0.3	750			
	2,700	0.2	540			
	2,800	0.3	840	2,530	0.756	1,913
3.	1,500	0.1	150			
	2,200	0.1	220			
	2,800	0.7	1,960			
	3,500.	0.1	350	2,680	0.658	1,763
				NPV		{584

As the NPV of the proposal is negative, the proposal is not acceptable

X Ltd. is evaluating two equal size mutually exclusive proposals A and B for which the respective cash flows together with associated probabilities are as follows :

Year 1		Year 2	
Cash Flows (Rs.)	**Prob.**	**Cash Flows**	**Prob.**
2,000		1,000	0.1
4,000		3,000	0.1
6,000		5,000	0.4
		7,000	0.3
		9,000	0.1

Find out the risks of the proposals in terms of the standard deviation.

Solution :

1. The expected monetary value of cash flows of project X and Y may be calculated as follow:.

Project X = 2,000 (0.3) + 4,000 {0.4} + 6,000 (0.3)

= Rs. 4,000 Project Y = 1,000 (0.1) + 3000(0.1) + 5,000(0.4) + 7,000(0.3) + 9,000(0.1)

= Rs. 5,400 on the basis of return, project Y is preferable as it gives higher return.

2.Calculation of standard deviations

Project X				Project Y			
CF (Rs.)	EMV.	Prob.	P(CF-EMV)^2	CF (Rs)	EMV.	Prob.	P(CF - EMV)^2
2,000	4,000	0.3	12,00,000	1,000	5,400	0.1	19,36,000
4,000	4,000	0.3	0	3,000	5,400	0.1	5,76,000
6,000	4,000	0.3	12,00,000	5,000	5,400	0.4	64,000
				7,000	5,400	0.3	7,68,000
				9,000	5,400	0.1	12,96,000
			24,00,000				46,40,000

Risk i.e. SD_x = “24,00,000 = 1,549;

SDy = “46,40,000 = 2,154

On the basis of risk project *x* is preferable as risk is low.

The above evaluation shows Project *x* — less return less risk

y — high return high risk

To resolve the dilemma in decision-making coefficient of variation is used

CV = SD / EMV

CV*x* = 1549/ 4000 = 0.287

CV*y* = 2,154 / 5400 = 0.398

Project *Y* has a higher CV of 0.398 and hence is more risky. Hence project *x* is preferable.

Example 5. *The R and Co. is engaged in evaluating the following mutually exclusive proposals, P1 and P2, for which the relevant information is as follows:*

Proposal P1		Proposal P2	
Cash Flows (Rs.)	"Prob.	Cash Flows	Prob.
7,50,000	0.3	-4,00,000	0.2
2,00,000	0.3	3,00,000	0.6
2,50,000	0.4	4,00,000	0.7
		8,00,000	0.7

Evaluate the proposals in terms of the standard deviation and coefficient of variation

Solution :

The expected value of cash flows (EMV) may be calculated as follows :

Prop. PI = (1,50,000 x 0.3) + (2,00,000 x 0.3) + (2,50,000 x 0.4) = 2,05,000

Prop. P2 = (-4,00,000) 0.2 + (3,00,000) 0.6 + 4,00,000 (0.1) + 8,00,000 (0.1) = 2,20,000

EVALUATION OF PROPOSALS

Proposal PI (Rs. '000)			Proposal P2 (Rs. '000)		
CFAT (Rs.)	Prob. (p)	P (CFAT - EMV)^2	CFAT (Rs.)	Prob. (P)	P (CFAT - EMV)^2
150	0.3	907.5	-400	0.2	76,880
200	0.3	7.5	300	0.6	3,840
250	0.4	810.0	400	0.1	3,240
			800	0.1	33,640
		1,725.0			1,17,600

Expected Monetary value
i.e. EMV return = 205 220

Now, the standard deviation and CV of the proposals are :

Proposal PI		Proposal P2
$(1,752)^{1/2} = 41.53$		$(1,17,600)^{1/2} = 342.93$
or SD	Rs. 41,530	*Rs.* 3,42,930
CV(i.e., SD/EMV)	0.20	1.56

Proposal 1 has lower risk (0.2) when compared to proposal 2 (1.56).

Hence proposal 1 should be preferred.

Example 6. *There are 5 projects A, B, C, D, E*

Project A has an expected return of 12% with a standard duration of 3%.

Project B has an expected return of 13% with a standard duration of 3.5%.

Project C has an expected return of 15% with a standard duration of 4%.

Project D has an expected return of 15.5% with a standard duration of 4.5%.

Project E has an expected return of 17% with a standard duration of 6%.

From the above information you are required to compare the projects and say which is the most risky project and which is the least risky project. ***(June 2007)***

Solution :

Project	Return (x)	SD	CV(SD/X)	
A	12	3	0,25	Least risky project
B	13	3.5	0.27	
C	15	4	0.267	
D	15.5	4.5	0.29	
E	17	6	0.353	Most risky project

(b) Risk and Return in Portfolio Context :

The following are the measures for risk and return in port' folio context

(1) Risk & Return of Single Asset :

The single period rate of return for an asset is given by

$$r = \frac{\text{Annual income + Capital Appreciation}}{\text{Purchase price of the satrt of the period}}$$

The expected rate of return is given by

$$E(r) = \sum_{t=1}^{n} P_t r_t$$

$E(r)$ = Expected return r_t = return P_t = Probability n = Possible rates of return. The variability of return i.e., risk is measured by

$$\text{Standard deviation } (\sigma) = \sqrt{\sum_{t=1}^{n} [r_t - E(r)]^2 P_t}$$

***(ii)* Risk and Return of a Portfolio :** A portfolio means a combination of two/more securities (assets). As investors construct a portfolio of investments rather invest in a single asset, this section extends the analysis of risk and return associated with single investment to portfolio investments.

(*a*)Portfolio Expected Return : The expected return on a portfolio is the weighted average of the expected returns of the securities comprising the portfolio. The weights are equal to the proportion of total funds in each security. Symbolically, the expected return of a portfolio, r_p.

$$r_P = \sum_{t=1}^{n} W_j r_j$$

Where Wj = the proportion invested in security j. rj = expected, return for security j. n = total number of securities in the portfolio, 'the weights must sum to 1, $\Sigma W_j = 1$

To illustrate, the expected returns for two securities, X and Y, are 16 and 21 per cents respectively. If the proportion of portfolio invested in the two securities are 0.35 and 0,65, the expected portfolio return = [(0.35) × 0.16 + (0.65) × 0.12] = 0.134 or 13.4 per cent.

(*b*) Portfolio Risk : Portfolio is the combination of different securities. The correction is also a measure of the relationship between two assets. The correlation coefficient can take on a value from –1 to +1. Correlation and covariance are related. Covariance is a statistical measure of how the return of two assets move together.

$$\text{Cov}_{12} = \sigma_1 \sigma_2 P_{12}$$

$$P_{12} = \frac{COV_{12}}{\sigma_1 \sigma_2}$$

$$\sigma_p = \sqrt{W_1^2 \sigma_1^2 + W_2^2 \sigma_2^2 + 2W_1 W_2 P_{12} \sigma_1 \sigma_2}$$

Where σ_1, σ_2 = S.D. of returns of assets 1 and 2

ρ_{12} = Correlation .coefficient of assets 1 and 2. W_1, W_2 = Weights of assets 1 and 2.

(*c*) Decision Tree Approach : The decision tree approach (DT) is another useful alternative for evaluating risky investment proposals. The outstanding feature of this method is that it takes into account the impact of all probabilistic estimates of potential outcomes. In other words, every possible outcome is weighed in probabilistic terms and then evaluated. The DT approach is especially useful for situations in which decisions at one point of time also affect the decisions of the firm at some later date. Another useful application of the DT approach is for projects which require decisions to be made is sequential parts.

A decision tree is a pictorial representation in tree form which indicates the magnitude, probability and inter-relationship of all possible outcomes. The format of the exercise of the investment decision has an appearance of a tree with branches and, therefor, this method is referred to as the decision tree method. A decision tree shows the sequential cash flows and the NPV of the proposed project under different circumstances.

DT figures covers all the dimensions of the problem

1. Timing of cash flows.
2. The possible cash flows outcomes in each year and
3. The probabilities associated with these outcomes.

Steps *in Decision tree Approach :*

1. Break the project into clearly defined stages.
2. Chart out all possible outcomes with probabilities of each outcome at different stages on the basis of available information.
3. Specify the effect of each outcome on expected cash flows from the project.
4. Evaluate the optimal action to be taken at each stage based on outcomes at the previous stage and its effect on cash flows.
5. Estimate the optimal action to be taken at the very first stage based on expected cash flows over the entire projects and all likely outcomes of the cash flows.

The expected NPV (NPV) of the project under decision tree approach is given by

$$\overline{NPV} = \sum_{\rho_j=1}^{m} P_j NPV_j \text{ i.e.,}$$

$$\text{Expected NPV} = \sum_{\text{Path}} \text{Joint probability} \times \text{NPV}$$

The sum of the joint probabilities must be equal to 1 always.

Decision Rule : The decision would be to accept the project of the sum of weighted-NPVs is positive else reject the project. This is also called as sum rule as the decision is based on total of weighted NPVs

Merits

1. It exhibits a birds eye view of all possibilities associated with proposed project
2. It makes management aware of all adverse possibilities in advance.
3. It shows conditional nature of CFAT associated with the project

Demerits : DT format becomes very unwidely, complex and difficult to understand and construct if the number of years of life of the project, number of possible outcomes for each year are large.

Example 1. *Suppose a firm has an investment proposal, requiring an outlay of Rs, 2,00,000 at present (t =0). The investment proposal is expected to have 2 year's economic life with no salvage value. In year 1, there is a 0.3 probability that CFAT will be Rs. 80,000; a 0.4 probability that CFAT will be Rs.1,10,000 and a 0.3 probability that CFAT will be Rs. 1,50,000. In year 2 the CFA T possibilities depend on CFAT that occurs in year 1. That is, the CFAT of the year 2 are conditional on CFAJ for the year 1. Accordingly, the probabilities assigned with the CFAT of the year 2 are conditional probabilities. The estimated conditional CFAT and their associated conditional probabilities are as follows:*

Solution :

If CFAT = Rs. 80,000		If CFAT = 1,10,000		If CFAT=Rs. 1,50,000	
CFAT1 Rs.	Probability	$CFAT_2$ Rs.	Probability	$CFAT_3$ Rs.	Probability
40,000	0.2	7,30,000	0.3	7,60,000	0.1
7,00,000	0.6	7,50,000	0.4	2,00,000	0.8
7,50,000	0.2	7,60,000	0.3	2,40,000	0.1

Time : 0	Year 1 Rs.		Year 1 Rs.		Path	Expected. NP Vat 12% Rs.	Joint Prob, Rs.	Expected NPV (x) Pj Rs.
	Prob.	CFAT	Prob.	CFAT		WN 1	WN2	
			0.2	40,000	1	(–96,680)	0.06	(–5,800.8)
	0.3	80,000	0.6	1,00,000	2	(–48,860)	0.18	(–8,796.8)
			0.2	1,50,000	3	(–9,010)	0.06	(–540.6)
			0.3	1,30,000	4	1,840	0.12	210.8
Cash	Q.4	1,10,000	0.4	1,50,000	5	17,780	0.16	2,844.8
outlays			0.3	1,60,000	6	25,750	0.12	3.090.0
Rs.2			0.1	1,60,000	7	61,470	0.03	1,844.1
LAC	0.3	1,50,000	0.8	2,00,000	8	93,350	0.24	22,404.0
			0.1	2,40,000	9	1,25,230	0.03	3,756.9
							1	**19,024.4**

Working Notes : 1. Calculations of NPV's

Year	CFAT			PV factor	PVCFAT		
	Path 1	Path 2	Path 3	©12%	Path -1	Path - 2	Path -3
0	(2,00,000)	(2,00,000)	(2,00,000)	1.000	(2,00,000)	(2,00,000)	(2,00,000)
1	80,000	80,000	80,000	0.893	71,440	71,440	71,440
2	40,000	1,00,000	1,50,000	0.797	31,880	79,700	1,19,550
			NPV		96,680	48,860	9,010

2. Calculation of Joint Probabilities and NPV's

Path	Joint Probabilities
1	0.3 x 0.2 = 0.06
2	0.3 x 0.6 - 0.18
3	0.3 x 0.2 - 0.06

Similar is the calculation of NPV's and joint probabilities for other paths Decision :

1. Since the sum of weighted NPV's is positive, Accept the project.
2. The project yields - 96,680 NPV of worst outcome is realized and 0.06 is the probability of occurrence of this NPV.
3. 1,25,230 NPV is the best outcome with 0.03 probability of occurrence.

CAPITAL BUDGETING DECISIONS UNDER CAPITAL RATIONING

In a situation where the firm has unlimited funds, all independent investment proposals — yielding return greater than some predetermined level are accepted; Business firms in actual practice have a fixed capital budget. A large number of investment proposals compete for these limited funds. The firm must, therefore, ration them. The firm allocates funds to projects in a manner that it maximizes long-run returns. Thus, capital rationing refers to a situation in which a firm has more acceptable investments than it can finance. It is concerned with the selection of a group of investment proposals out of many investment proposals acceptable under the accept-reject decision. Capital rationing employs ranking of the acceptable investment projects. The projects can be ranked on the basis of a predetermined criterion such as the rate of return.

Capital Rationing is of two Types

1. Internal Capital Rationing : The firm may follow a policy of using internally generated funds for new investments or has a limit on funds allocated for fresh investments so as to avoid debt capital and thereby financial risk and avoid external equity and there by do not lose control such situation is referred to internal capital rationing.

2. External Capital Rationing : The firm may be willing to undertake the financially label proposals but do not have sufficient funds at its disposal or capital market conditions are not conducive enough to raise required funds from the market for reasons like lack of credibility high flotation costs and high cost of capital. Such situation is referred, to external capital rationing.

Conclusion : The risk dimension in capital budgeting cannot be ignored, profitability and risk are closely related. It is very likely that a project which is potentially very profitable may also increase the perceived risk of the firm. This trade-off between risk and profitability would have a bearing on the investor's perception of the firm before and after the acceptance of a specific proposal. If the acceptance of a proposal, for instance, makes a firm more risky, the investors would not look to it with favour. This may have an adverse implication for the market price of shares, total valuation of the firm and its goal. It is therefore necessary to incorporate the risk factor in the analysis of capital budgeting.

CHAPTER 3

Financing Decisions

A. Capital Structure

Sources of Finance for Entrepreneurs

A project is a productive activity which can be analyzed, appraised and monitored independently.

Finance is one of the basic requirements of a project. The entrepreneur needs capital to-start with and one needs financial assistance at every stage of the project. Project finance is both for short-term and long-term. The sources from which the entrepreneurs can need their financial needs for their projects are : internal source and external source. Besides, the entrepreneur raises his finance by availing of available subsidies, state aid to industries, etc. Project finance, therefore, is very crucial for the success of a project.

Finance is one of the constant problems, and if the economy has to develop in the way the Government policy hopes, various segments such as agriculture, industry, transport etc., must have a adequate credit. Credit is available on the basis of the credit worthiness of the entrepreneur. In regard to capital structure and working capital management, substantial differences between large, medium and small-scale industries exist.

Finance is. the catalyst agent for development. Finance is the life-blood of any business. Its management is an art and merits separate attention. The financial function of management is to : .

(a) Ensure fair returns on investments;

(b) Generate and build surpluses and reserves for growth and expansion;

(c) Plan, direct and control the utilization of finances so as to ensure maximum efficiency of operations.

(d) Co-ordinate the operations of the various departments through appropriate measure.

Depending upon the nature of the activity, the entrepreneurs require three types of finances. The distinctive features of these are emulated below :

1. Short-Term Finance

Short-term finance usually refers to funds required for a period of less than one year. These funds are usually required to meet variable, seasonal or temporary, working capital requirements.

Borrowing from banks is a very important source of short-term finance. Other important sources of short-term finance are trade credit, installment credit and customer advances.

2. Medium-Term Finance

The period of one year to five years may be regarded as a medium-term. Medium-term finance is usually required for permanent working capital, small expansions, replacements, modifications etc.

Medium-term finance may be raised by 0) issue of shares; issue of debentures; borrowing from banks and other financial institutions; and plouging back of Profits.

3. Long-Term Finance

The period exceeding 5 years is regarded as long-term. Long-term finance is required for procuring fixed assets, for the establishment of a new business, for substantial expansion of existing business, modernization etc.

The important sources of long-term finance are similar to the medium-term finance to industry.

Types of Finance

Short-Term	Medium-Term	Long-Term
1. Bank credit 2. Trade credit	1. Issue of shares 2. Issue of debentures	1. Issue of shares 2. Issue of debentures
3. Instalment credit	3. Loads from banks and other financial Institutions	3. Loans from financial institutions
4. Customer advances	4. Public deposits (for existingconcerns)	4. Ploughing back of profits (forexisting concerns)
	5. Ploughing back of profits (for existing concerns)	

A characteristic feature of manufacturing units/ entrepreneurs that the personal funds of entrepreneurs form a substantial proportion of the total assets. Most of the units are not corporate entities. The owners of small units, therefore, run a considerably higher risk than those of corporate units. The sources that usually provide the working capital requirements are commercial banks, special agencies like the State Industrial and Investment Corporation of Maharashtra (SICOM), and the Gujarat Industrial Investment Corporation (GIIC), and operative banks, Indigenous bankers and moneylenders also advance loan for working capital needs. The fixed capital needs are usually met by State Governments (under the State Aid (to Industries Acts/Rules), State Financial Corporations (SFCs), National Small Industries Corporation (NSIC), State Small Industries Corporations (SSICs), State Industrial Development Corporations (SIDCs) and Commercial banks and other financial institutions and is presented below :

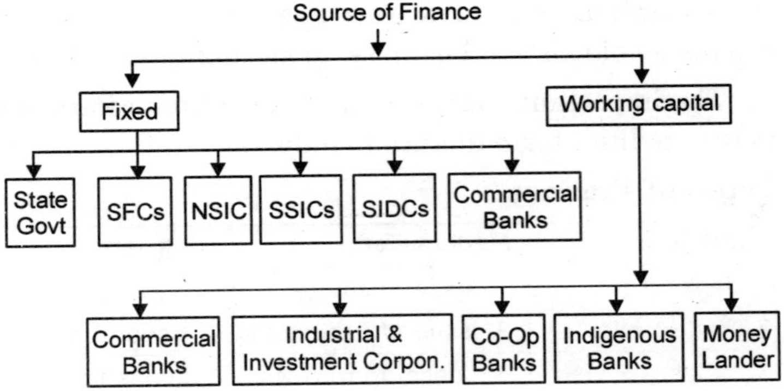

Sources of Long-Term External Finances

The main sources of long-term finance fall into two broad groups :

A. External i.e., equity capital preference capital, debentures, and term loans.

B. Internal i.e., retained earnings.

A. EXTERNAL SOURCE OF FINANCING

1. Equity Share Capital : Ownership capital and its owners, i.e., ordinary or equity share holders share the reward and risk associated with ownership of corporate enterprises. It is also called as ***ordinary share capital.***

Features

(a) The equity shareholders have residual claim to the income and assets of the company.

(b) They have indirect right to control the operations of the company by exercising voting rights.

(c) The equity shareholders enjoy pre-emptive rights to acquire 2% of the additional shares to be issued by the company. The option to the share holders to purchase a specified number of shares at a stated price during a given period is called rights.

(*i*) *Rights Issue are* the shares issued to the existing shareholders of a company at a subscription price i.e., generally lower than current share price. The shareholders proportionate ownership remains unchanged when the rights are exercised. When rights are issued, the share will increase leading to dilution in EPS, DPS, Book value and MPS.

In short, equity is high cost and low/nil risk permanent source of long-term finance for performing corporate enterprises.

(*ii*) *Sweat Equity :* These are the shares issued by the company to its employees at a price lower than the ...market price as a reward for best performance ...employees.

(*ii*) All unpaid dividends are carri... before any ordinary dividend is paid.

(*iii*) It can be retired on maturity and can be convertible partly or fully into equity shares. Preference capital also carries high cost with negligible risk like equity capital.

3. Debenture Capital

Debenture holders are long-term creditors to the company. Equity capital has got variable income i.e., dividends while debenture capital has got fixed income i.e., interest.

Feature's

(*i*) It can be redeemed after maturity period or can also convertible into equity shares.

(*ii*) The debenture holder have claim on income as it is a contractual obligation enforceable by law.

Debentures have low cost and low risk and tax-deducibility of interest with no dilution of control and voting rights. But the increased financial risk will increase the cost of equity.

Capital Structure

Introduction

The assets of a company can be financed either by increasing the owner's claims or the creditor's claims. The owner's claims increase when the firm raises funds by issuing ordinary shares or by retaining the earning's; the creditor's claims increase by borrowing. The various means of financing represent the financial structure of an enterprise. The term capital structure is used to represent the proportionate relationship between debt and equity. Equity includes paid up share capital, share premium and reser (retained earnings).

Importanc

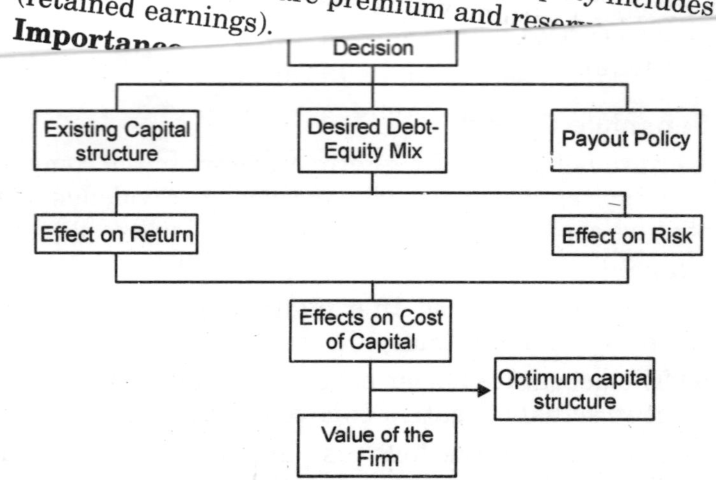

The Capital Structure Decision Process

The financing or capital structure decision is a significant managerial decision as it influences the shareholder's return and risk. Consequently, the market value of the share may be affected by the capital structure decision. The company will have to plan its capital structure initially at the time of its promotion. Subsequently, whenever funds have to be raised to finance investments, a capital structure decision is involved. The process of the capital structure decision is shown below.

A demand for raising funds generates a new capital structure since a decision has to be made as to the quantity and forms of financing. This decision will involve an analysis, of the existing capital structure and the factors which will govern the decision at present. The dividend decision is also a financing decision. The company's policy to retain or distribute earnings affects the owner's claims. Shareholder's equity position is strengthened by retention of earnings. Thus, the dividend decision has a bearing on the capital structure of the company. The new financing decision of the company may affect its debt-equity mix. The debt-equity mix has implications for the shareholder's earnings and risk, which in turn, will affect the cost of capital and the market value of the firm. The capital structure is optimum when the value of the firm is maximum and the cost of capital is minimum i.e., trade off point between risk and return.

Thus, capital structure refers to the mix of long term sources of funds, such as debentures, long term debt, preference share capital and equity share capital including reserves and surplus and retained earnings.

A sound *of appropriate capital structure should have the following features :*

- **Return :** The capital structure of the company should be most advantageous. Subject to other considerations, it should generate maximum returns to the shareholders without adding additional cost to them.

- **Risk :** The use of excessive debt threatens the solvency of the company. The debt does not add significant risk, upto a point and later risk increases at that point debt should be avoided.
- **Flexibility :** The capital structure should be flexible. It should be possible for a company to adapt its capital structure with a minimum cost and delay if warranted by a changed situation.
- **Capacity :** The capital structure be determined within the debt capacity, of the company, and this capacity should not be exceeded.
- **Control :** The capital structure should involve minimum risk of loss of control of the company.

Types of Leverage and Their Determination

The following are the different types of leverage important in financial decision-making.

Leverage is an important aspect to be understood. The concept of leverage in financial analysis reflects the responsiveness or influence of one financial variable over some other financial variable.

There are three types of leverages, operating, financial and combined leverages.

OPERATING LEVERAGE

Operating leverage affects a firm's operating profit (EBIT), while financial leverage affects profit after tax or the earnings per share. The combined affect of two leverages can be quite significant for the earnings available to ordinary shareholders.

Degree of Operating Leverage : The degree of operating leverage (DOL) was defined as the percentage change in the earnings before interest and taxes relative to a given percentage change in sales. Thus:

DOL = CONTRIBUTION/EBIT

For example *X* Ltd. management had developed the following income statement based on an expected sales volume of 1,00,000 units :

	Rs.
Sales (1,00,000 units at Rs. 8)	8,00,000
Less : Variable costs (1,00,000 at Rs. 4)	4.00.000
Contribution	4,00,000
Less : Fixed costs	2.80.000
EBIT	1.20.000

	Rs.
Sales (1,00,000 units at Rs. 8)	8,00,000
Less : Variable costs (1,00,000 at Rs. 4)	4.00.000
Contribution	4,00,000
Less : Fixed costs	2.80.000
EBIT	1.20.000

Applying equation (ii), DOL is :

$$DOL = \frac{100,000(8-4)}{100000(8-4) - 280,0000} = 3.33$$

DOL of 3.33 implies that for a given change in *X Ltd.*, sales, EBIT will change by 3.33 times.

FINANCIAL LEVERAGE

Degree of Financial Leverage

Financial leverage affects the earnings per share. When the economic conditions are good and the firm's EBIT is increasing, its EPS increases faster with more debt in the capital structure. The degree of financial leverage (DFL) is defined as the percentage change in EPS due to a given percentage change in EBIT :

DFL = EBIT / EBIT – INT = EBIT/ PBT

COMBINED LEVERAGE

Operat'ng and financial leverage together cause wide

fluctuation in EPS for a given change in sales. If a company employs a high level of operating and financial leverage, even a small change in the level of sales will have dramatic effect on EPS.

The degree of combined leverage (DCL) is given by the following equation :

DCL = CONTRIBUTION/PBT

Sensitivity of EPS to EBIT

For an appropriate capital structure it is important to understand how sensitive is EPS (Earnings Per Share) to changes in EBIT (earnings before interest and taxes) for share under different financing alternatives.

One of the objectives of planning an appropriate capital structure is to provide a high income for the equity owners, that is, to increase the EPS. To device an appropriate capital structure or financing plan, the amount of EBIT under various financing plans should be related to EPS. Thus, one widely used means of examining the effect of leverage is to analyze the relationship between EBIT and EPS.

1. EBIT-EPS Analysis : The EBIT-EPS analysis studies the effect of leverage, and involves the comparison of alternative methods of financing under various assumptions of EBIT, A firm has the choice to raise funds for financing its investment proposals from different sources in different proportions. A firm can (*i*) exclusively use equity capital; (*ii*) exclusively use debt; (*iii*) exclusively use preference capital; (*iv*) use a combination of above in different proportions. The choice of the combination of the various sources would be one which, given the level of earnings before interest and taxes, would ensure the largest EPS.

Earning per Share = Profit after tax / Number of share

EPS of Debt-Equity plan (levered firm) = PAT / N = (EBIT – I)(I-T) / N

Where T is the corporate tax rate and N is the number

ordinary shares outstanding. If the firm does not employ any debt, then the formula simply would be :

EPS of Equity plan (Unlevered firm)

$$= EBIT(1-T)\ /N \qquad — (I = 0;\ if\ D = 0)$$

If a company uses equity, preference capital and debt then EPS may be calculated as follows:

$$EPS = (EBIT - I)\ (1 - T) - D_P\ /N$$

Important Consideration

1. *Dp* the preference dividend, is not tax deductible.
2. Levered firm is firm with debt financing and thereby incur interest burden.
3. Unlevered firm is firm without debt financing in its capital structure.

2. Indifference Point : The level of EBIT at which EPS would be the same under both the plans is known as indifference point. The break even level of EBIT can be arrived by equating EPS of two plans.

For e.g. : equity plan to debt - equity plans

$EBIT\ (1\text{-}t)/N_1 = (EBIT - I)\ (1 - t)/\ N_2$

Debt - equity plan to preference, debt and equity plans

$EBIT\ (1\text{-}t)/N_1 = (EBIT - I)\ (1 - t) - DP/N_2$

Similarly different capital structure plans can be equated to get a break even EBIT. In short this is the level of EBIT where EPS of plans would be equal.

FINANCIAL LEVERAGE — IMPACT ON SHARE HOLDERS RETURN AND RISK

Meaning of Financial Leverage

The use of the fixed-charges sources of funds, such as debt and preference capital along with the owner's equity in the capital structure, is described as financial leverage or gearing or trading on equity. The use of the term trading on equity is derived from the fact that it is the owner's equity that is used as a basis to raise debt; that is, the equity that is traded upon.

The financial leverage employed by a company is intended to earn more on the fixed charges funds than their costs. The surplus (or deficit) will increase (or decrease) the return on the owner's equity. The rate of return on the owner's equity is levered above or below the rate of return on total assets.

(a) Measure of Financial Leverage : ***The most commonly used measures of financial leverage are* :**

1. Debt Ratio : The ratio of debt to total capital, i.e., D/D+S = D/V

Where D is value of debt, S is value of equity and *V is* value of total capital. D and S may be measured in terms of book value or market value. The book value of equity is called net worth.

2. Debt-Equity Ratio : The ratio of debt to equity, i.e., D/S

3. Interest Coverage : The ratio of net operating income (or EBIT) to interest charges, i.e., EBIT/ *Interest*

The first two measure of financial leverage, are also measures of capital gearing.

The third measure of financial leverage, commonly known as coverage ratio, The reciprocal of interest coverage, that is interest divided by EBIT, is a measure of the firm's income gearing.

(*b*) Financial Leverage and The Shareholder's Return : The primary motive of a company in using financial leverage is to magnify the shareholder's return under favourable economic conditions. The role of financial leverage in magnifying the return of the shareholders is based on the assumptions that the fixed-charges funds (such as the loan from financial Institutions and other sources or debentures) can be obtained at a cost lower than the firm's rate of return on net assets (RONA or ROI):. It should, therefore, be understood that EPS, ROE and ROI are the important figures for analyzing the impact of financial leverage.

(*c*) Financial "Leverage and Shareholders Risk : Financial leverage magnifies the shareholder's earnings. The variability of EBIT causes EPS to fluctuate within wider ranges with debt in the capital structure. That is, with more debt, EPS rises and falls faster than the rise and fall in EBIT. Thus, financial leverage not only magnifies EPS but also increases its variability.

The variabilities of EBIT and EPS distinguish between two types of risk-operating risk and financial risk. The distinction between operating and financial risk is explained below:

Operating Risk : Operating risk can be defined as the variability of EBIT {or return on total assets). The environment-internal and external-in which a firm operates determines the variability of EBIT.

Financial Risk: For a given degree of variability of EBIT, the variability of EPS increases with more financial leverage. The variability of EPS caused by the use of financial leverage is called *financial risk.*

CAPITAL STRUCTURE AND VALUE OF THE FIRM

Introduction

Given a certain level of earnings, the value of the firm is maximized when the cost of capital is minimized and vice versa.

There is considerable effect of leverage on the shareholder's earnings and risk. Under favourable economic conditions, the earnings per share increase with leverage. But leverage also increases the financial risk of the shareholders. Hence, the objective of a firm should be directed towards the maximization of the value of the firm and the capital structure or leverage decisions should be examined from the point of its impact on the value of the firm. If the value of the firm can be affected by capital structure or financing decision, a firm would like to have a capital structure which maximizes the market value of the firm. There exist conflicting theories on the relationship between capital structure and the value of a firm. There exist two extreme views on optimum capital structure and value of the firm. David Durand identified the two extreme views — the net income and net operating approaches.

- **Net Income Approach:** Under the net income (NI) approach, the cost of debt and cost of equity are assumed to be independent to the capital structure. The weighted average cost of capital declines and the total value of the firm rises with increased use of leverage.
- **Net Operating Income Approach:** Under the net operating income (NOI) approach, the cost of equity is assumed to increase linearly with leverage. As a result, the weighted average cost of capital remains constant and the total value of the firm also remains constant as leverage is changed.
- **Traditional Approach:** According to this approach, the cost of capital declines and the value of the firm increases with leverage up to a prudent debt level and after reaching the optimum point {minimum cost of capital or maximum value of the firm), leverage causes the cost of capital to increase and the value of the firm to decline.

ASSUMPTION AND DEFINITIONS

In order to grasp the elements of the capital structure and the value of the firm or the cost of capital, the following assumptions are made :

- Firms employ only two types of capital: debt-and equity.

- The total assets of the firm are given. The degree of leverage can be changed by selling debt to repurchase shares or selling shares to retire debt.
- Investors have the same subjective probability distribution of expected future operating earning for a given firm.
- The firm as *a* policy of paying 100 per cent dividends.
- The operating earnings of the firm are not expected to grow.
- The business risk is assumed to be constant and independent of capital structure and financial risk.
- The corporate and personal income taxes do not exist,

Given the above assumptions, the analysis focuses on the following rates :

Kd = I / D = Annual interest Charges / Market value of debt

Assuming that the debt is perpetual rd represents the cost of debt.

Ke = E / S = Equity earnings / Market value of equity

When the dividend payout ratio is 100 per cent and earnings constant, rE, as defined here, represents the cost of equity.

Ko = O / V = Operating income / Market value of the firm

Where $V = D + E$. *ko* is the overall capitalization rate of the firm. Since it is the weighted average cost of capital, it may be expressed as follows :

$$Ko = Kd(D / D+S) + Ke(E / D+S)$$

In terms of above definitions, we analyze the change in *kD, Ke, kO* with the change in financial leverage *i.e., D / S*

Capital Structure Theories

1. Net Income Approach: According to this approach, the cost of debt, *kD,* and the cost of equity, *kE* remain unchanged when *D*/*S* varies. The constancy of *Kd* and *kE* with respect to *D*/*S* means that *kO,* the average cost of capital, declines as *D*/*E* increases. This happens because when *D*/*E* increases, *kD*. which is lower than *kE* receives a higher weight in the calculation of *kO*.

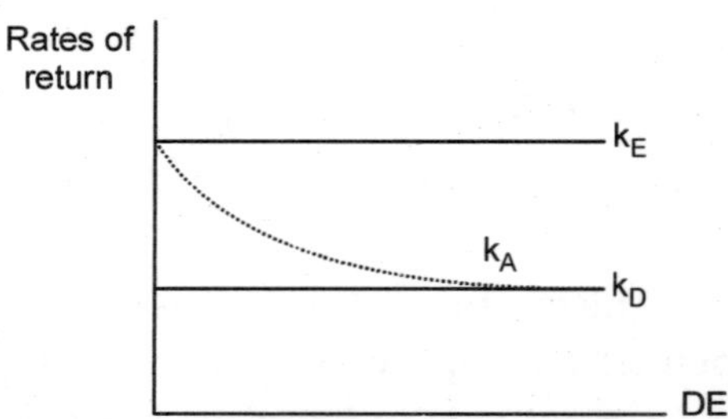

Behaviour of k_O, k_D and k_E as per Net Income Approach

As *D*/*S* increases, *Ko* decreases because the proportion of debt, the cheaper source of finance, increase in the capital structure.

Example 1. *The net income approach may be illustrated with a numerical example. There are two firms A and B similar in all aspects except in the capital structure employed by them. Financial data for these firms are shown below :*

		Firms A	Firm B
0	Operating income (EBIT)	Rs. 10,000	Rs. 10,000
I	Interest on debt	Rs. 0	Rs. 3,000
P_E	Equity earnings	Rs. 10,000	Rs. 7,000
k_E	Cost of equity capital	10%	10%
k_D	Cost of debt capital	6%	6%
ES	Market value of equity	Rs. 1,00,000	Rs. 70,000
D	Market value of debt	Rs. 0	Rs. 50,000
V	Total value of the firm	Rs. 1,00,000	Rs. 1,20,000

The average cost of capital for firm A is *(ko)*

*6% * 0/100000 + 10% * 100 000/100 000 = 10%*

The average cost of capital for firm *B is (ko)*

6% * 50000/120000 + 10% 70000/100000

Net Operating Income Approach : According to the net operating income approach, the overall capitalization rate and the cost of debt remain constant for all degrees of leverage. In the equation.

$$k_O = k_D\left[\frac{D}{D+S}\right] + k_E\left[\frac{E}{D+S}\right]$$

k_o and kD are constant for all degrees of leverage. Given this, the cost of equity can be expressed as :

$$k_E = k_O + (k_0 - k_D)\frac{D}{E}$$

The above behaviour of kD, kE and k_Q in response to changes in (D/S) is shown graphically below :

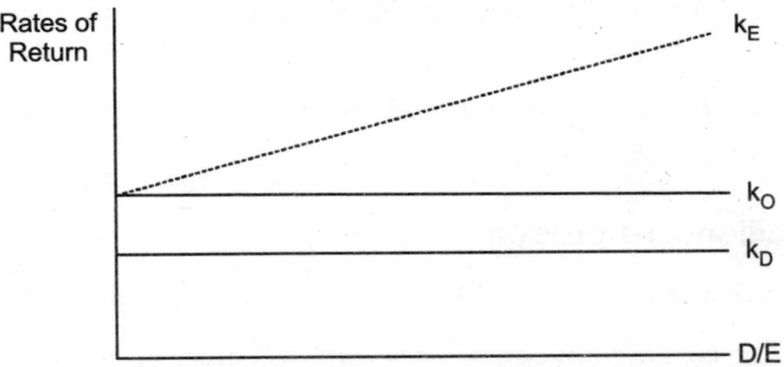

Behaviour of k_0, k_D, and k_E as per the Net Operating Income Approach

The critical premise of this approach is that the market capitalizes the firm as a whole at a discount rate which is independent of the firm's debt-equity ratio. As a consequence, the division between debt and equity is irrelevant. An increase in the use of debt funds which are 'cheaper' is offset by an increase in the equity capitalization rate. This happens because equity investors seek higher compensation as they are exposed to greater risk arising from increasing in the degree of leverage.

Example 2. *Two firms A and B, are similar in all respects except the financial leverage employed by them. Relevant financial data for these firms are shown below :*

		Firms A	Firm B
0	Net operating Income	10,000	10,000
KO	Overall capitalization rate	0.15	0.15
V	Total market value	66,667	66,667
I	Interest on debt	1,000	3,000
ko	Debt capitalization rate	0.10	0.10
D	Market value of debt	10,000	30,000
ES	Market value of equity	56,667	36,667
D/S	Financial leverage	0.176	0.818

The equity capitalization rates of firms *A* and *B* are as follows :

FIRM *A* : Equity earnings/Market value of equity = 9000/ 56667 = 15.9 %

FIRM *B* : Equity earnings/Market value of equity = 7000/ 36667 = 19.10%

3. Traditional Approach

The main propositions of the *traditional approach are :*

(*i*) The cost of debt capital, ***kD*** remains more or less constant up to a certain degree of leverage but rises thereafter at an increasing rate.

(*ii*) The cost of equity capital, ***kE***, remains more or less constant or rises only gradually up to a certain degree of leverage and rises sharply thereafter.

(*iii*) The average cost of capital, ***kO*** consequence of the above behaviour of ***kE*** and K_0, (*a*) decreases up to certain point; (*b*) remains more or less unchanged for moderate increases in leverage thereafter; and (*c*) rises beyond a certain point.

The traditional approach is not as sharply defined as the net income approach or the net operating income approach. This approach is illustrated graphically.

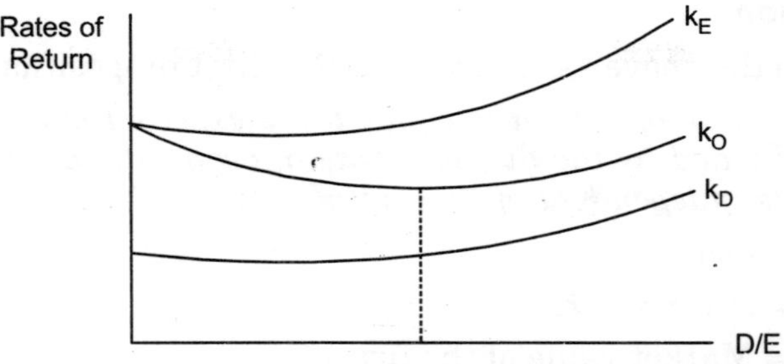

Behaviour of k_0, k_D, and k_E Under the Traditional Approach

The principal implication of the traditional position is that the cost of capital is dependent on the capital structure and there is an optimal capital structure which minimizes the cost of capital.

Criticism of the Traditional Approach : The traditional view is criticized because it implies that totality of risk incurred by all security-holders of a firm can be altered by changing the way in which this totality of risk is distributed among the various classes of securities.

4. Modigliani and Miller Approach (MM Approach) : Assumption :

The following are the assumptions underlying the MM propositions :

- *Perfect Capital Market:* Information is freely available and there is no problem of asymmetric information; transactions are costless; there are not bankruptcy costs; securities are infinitely divisible.
- *Rational Investors and Managers :* Investors rationally choose a combination of risk and return that is most advantageous to them. Managers act in the interest of shareholders'
- *Homogeneous Expectations :* Investors hold identical expectations about future operating earnings.
- *Equivalent Risk Classes :* Firms can be grouped into 'equivalent risk classes' or. the basis of their business risk.
- *Absence of Taxes :* There is no tax.

Proposition I

Based on the above assumptions, MM's first proposition is ;

"The *value of a firm is equal to its expected operating income divided by the discount rate appropriate to its risk class. It is independent of its capital structure*".

In symbols

$$V = D + S = O/K.$$

where V = Market value of the firm

D = Market value of debt

S = Market value of equity

O = Expected operating income

k = Discount rate applicable to the risk class to which the firm belongs

Proposition I is identical to the net operating income approach. MM invoked an arbitrage argument to prove this proposition. In equilibrium, identical assets must sell for the same price, irrespective of how they are financed.

ARBITRAGE ARGUMENT

To know the arbitrage mechanism works, consider two firms, U and L, similar in all respects except in their capital structure. Firm U is an unlevered firm financed by equity alone, whereas firm L is a levered firm financed by a mix of equity and debt. Relevant financial particulars of the two firms are shown below :

	Firms A	Firm B
Operating Income (EBIT)	1,50,000	1,50,000
Interest	0	60,000
Equity earnings	1,50,000	90,000
Cost of equity	0.15	0.16
Market value of equity	10,00,000	5,62,500
Cost of debt	–	0.12
Market value of debt	0	5,00,000
Market value of the firm	10,00,000	10,62,500
Average cost of capital	0.15	0.1412

According to above table, the value of the levered firm *L* is higher than that of the unlevered firm even though both the firms have the same operating income and belong to the same risk. Such a situation, cannot persist because equity investors would do well to sell their equity in firm *L* (the firm which is values more) and invest in firm *U* (the firm which is valued less) with personal leverage. For example, if an investor owns 10 per cent equity in firm *L*, he would do well to :

1. Sell his equity In firm L for Rs. 56,250.
2. Borrow Rs. 50,000, an amount equal to percent of L's debt, at an interest rate of 12 per cent.
3. Buy 10 per cent of firm U's equity for Rs. 1,00,000.

Investor collects Rs. 1,06,250 (Rs. 56,250 as sale proceeds of his equity plus Rs. 50,000 as borrowings), his investment is only Rs. 1,00,000, leaving him with a surplus amount of Rs, 6,250. Yet his income remains the same :

	Old Income from Investmꞈnt in L in U	New Income from from Investment in U
• 10% of firm's equity income	9,000	15,000
• 12% interest on Rs. 50,000 loan		(6,000)
	9,000	9,000

If the investor invests the surplus amount of 6,250 also, the new income will be greater than invested old income. The risk exposure remains unchanged as investor merely replaced personal borrowings to corporate borrowings, i.e., substitution of home made leverage for corporate leverage. Hence the value of unlevered *(VU)* from must be the same as the value of the levered from *(VL)* where

$$VL = VU.+ D\ (E)$$

Preposition - II : An increase in financial leverage increases the expected earnings per share but not the share price for the reason that the change in expected earnings is offset by corresponding change in the return required by the shareholders.

Expected return on assets is given by

$$kE = kO + (kO - kD)$$

The second proposition of MM expresses that "*the expected return on equity is equal to the expected rate of return on assets plus a premium. The premium is equal to the debt equity ratio times the difference between the expected return on assets and the expected return on debt*[1]'.

Important Considerations

1. *kO* is not affected by leverage because in perfect capital markets, leverage has no effect on firms operating income or market value of all securities.
2. In the investor owns all the firms debt and equity, entitling him all the operating income, the expected return on investors portfolio is equal to k_0.

Criticisms of MM theory

The leverage irrelevance theorem of MM is valid if the perfect market assumptions underlying their analysis are satisfied. The real world, however, is characterized by various imperfections.

- Firms are liable to pay taxes on their income.. In addition* investors who receive returns from their investments in firms are subject to taxes at a personal level.
- Bankruptcy costs can be quite high.
- Agency costs exist because of the conflict of interest between managers and shareholders and between shareholders and creditors.
- Managers seem to have a preference for a certain sequence of financing.
- Informational asymmetry exists because managers are better informed than investors.

- Personal leverage and corporate leverage are not perfect substitutes.

Conclusion : Proposition — I says that financial leverage has no effect on the wealth of shareholders and proposition II says that the rate of return expected by shareholder increases with financial leverage.

Shareholders are indifferent to increased leverage though it enhances expected return as there is accompanied increase in risk.

The capital structure of the firm has a bearing on valuation and firms do regard the capital structure decision as a major issue and thus the firms evaluate capital structure decisions in view of the Implications of these imperfections.

Examples 1. *Manufacturing company has a total capitalization of Rs. 10,00,000, and it normally earns Rs. 1,00,000 (before interest and taxes). The financial manager of the firm wants to take a decision regarding the capital structure. After a study of the capital market, he gathers the following data:*

Amount of Debt Rs.	Interest Rate %	Equity Capitalization Rate (at given level of debt) %
0	-	10.00
1,00,000	4.0	10.50
2,00,000	4.0	11.00
3,00,000	4.5	11.60
4,00,000	5.0	12.40
5,00,000	5.5	13.50
6,00,000	6.0	16.00
7,00,000	8.0	20.00

(a) What amount of debt should be employed by the firm if the traditional approach is held valid ?

(b) If the Modigliani - Miller approach is followed, what should be the equity capitalization rate ?

Solution : (a) As *per* the traditional approach, optimum capital structure exists when the weighted average cost of capital is minimum. The weighted average cost of capital calculations at book value weights are as follows :

k_E	W_E	k_D	W_D	$k_E W_E$	$k_D W_D$	k_0
(1)	(2)	(3)	(4)	(5)	(6)	(7) = (5) + (6)
0.100	1.0	-	-	0.1000	-	0.1000
0.105	0.9	0.040	0.1	0.0945	0.0040	0.0985
0.110	0.8	0.040	0.2	0.0880	0.0080	0.0960
0.116	0.7	0.045	0.3	0.0812	0.135	0.0947
0.124	0.6	0.050	0.4	0.0744	0.0200	0.0944
0.135	0.5	0.055	0.5	0.0675	Q.0275	0.0950
0.160	0.4	0.060	0.6	0.0640	0.0360	0.1000
0.200	0.3	0.080	0.7	0.0600	0.0560	0.1160

The firm should employ debt of Rs. 4,00,000 as the weighted average cost of capital is minimum at this level of debt

(b) Given '*ko* = 10 %, The equity rate is given by the following formula :

$$k_E = k_O + (k_O - k_D)\frac{D}{E}$$

The equity capitalization rates will be :

DebtRs.	k_D	ko		(ko - ko)	Debt/Equity	k_E
0	-	0.10	+	(0.10)	0	= 0.1000
1,00,000	0.040	0.10	+	(0.10-0.040)	1,00,000/9,00,000	= 0.1067
2,00,000	0.040	0,10	+	(0.10-0.040)	2,00,000/8,00,000	» 0.1150
3,00,000	0.045	0.10	+	(0.10-0.045)	3,00,000/7,00,000	– 0.1236
4,00,000	0.050	0.10	+	(0.10-0.050)	4,00,000/6,00,000	– 0.1333
5,00,000	0.050	0.10	+	(0.10-0.055)	5,00,000/5,00,000	* 0.1450
6,00,000	0.060	0.10	+	(0.10-0.060)	6,00,000/4,00,000	– 0.1600
7,00,000	0.080	0.10	+	(0.10-0.080)	7,00,000/3,00,000	= 0.1467

Example 2. *The following are the costs and values for the firms X and Y according to the traditional.*

	Firms X	Firm Y
Total value of firm, V	50,000	60,000
Market value of debt, D	0	30,000
Market value of Equity, 5	50,000	30,000
Expected net operating income, (EBIT)	5,000	5,000
Cost of debt, /NT- k_D D	0	1,800
Net income, E - EBIT-I	5,000	3,200
Cost of equity, /(£ - E/S	10. 00 %	10.70%
Debt - equity ratio, D/S	0	0.5
Average cost of capital, ko	10.00%	8.33%

Compute equilibrium value for firms X and Y in accordance with the M-M thesis. Assume that k_o is 9.09 per cent.

	Firms X	Firm Y
Expected net operating income (CBIT) D	5,000	5,000
Total cost of debt, INT = k_D D	0	1,800
Net Income D = (EBIT - 1)	5,000	3,200
Average cost of capital, k_0	0.909	0.909
Total value of firm, V = 0/ko	55,000	55,000
Market value of debt, D	0	30,000
Market value of shares, S = V - D	55,000	25,000
Cost of equity, Ke= 0/S	0.909	0.128

A company wants to build a new *plant costing Rs.* 10 *lacs. The funds can be raised through one of the following financial plans.*

(i) *Issue 7 lac equity shares at Rs. 10 per share.*

(ii) *Issue 50,000 equity shares at Rs. 10 per share, and 5,000 debentures of Rs. 100* each, *with an interest rate of 8% per annum.*

(iii) *Issue 50,000 equity shares at Rs. 10 per share, and 5,000 preference shares at Rs. 100* per share, *with a 9% rate of dividend.*

Calculate EPS under the 3 financing plans, when EBIT is (a) Rs. 40,000 (b) Rs, 200,000. The corporate tax rate is 50%. Which plan do you recommend for each level of EBIT ? ***(Sept 03),***

Solution :

1. Working Notes :

(A) Interest

Plan 1 : There is no debt, hence no interest.

Plan 2 : Debt = 5000 x R_s. 100 = 5,00,000.

Interest - 8% of 5,00,000 = Rs. 40,000.

Plan 3 : There is no debt, hence no interest

(B) Preference Dividend

Plan 1 : There are no preference shares hence no dividend.

Plan 2 : There are no preference shares hence no dividend.

Plan 3 : Preference capital = Rs. 5,00,000 × 9% * Rs. 45,000.

2.(a) Computation of EPS with EBIT * Rs. 40,000.

	Plan - 1	Plan - II	Plan - III
EBIT	40,000	40,000	40,000
(–) Interest WN (1)		40,000	-
EBT	40,000	-	40,000
(–) Tax (50%)	20,000	-	20,000
EAT	20,000	-	20,000
(-) Preference dividend WN (2) [P_D]			45,000
Earnings available to equity holders	20,000		-
No. of equity shares (N)	1,00,000	1,00,000	1,00,000
EPS	0.20	-	-

(b) Computation of EPS when EBIT = Rs. 2 lacs

	Plan - 1	Plan - II	Plan - III
EBIT	2,00,000	2,00,000	2,00,000
(–) Interest WN (1)	-	40,000	-
EBT	2,00,000	1,60,000	2,00,000
(–)Tax<50%)EAT	1,00,000 1,00,000	80,000 80,000	1,00,000 1,00,000
(–) Preference dividend WN (2)	-	-	45,000
Earnings available to equity holders	1,00,000	80,000	55,000
Divide by No. of eq. shares	1,00,000	50,000	50,000
EPS (Rs.)	1	1.60	1.10

Example 2. *XVZ Limited is an all equity firm which has an equity capital of Rs. 1,50,000, where the par value of a share is Rs. 10. The firm is in need of another Rs. 36,00,000 to finance its activities which would generate an EBIT of Rs. 9,00,000 after expansion. The finance manager had drawn the following three alternatives.*

Alternative — (i) : Raise the entire amount as equity.

Alternative — (ii): 50% of the required amount as equity and the remaining as debt @8% p.a.

Alternative — (iii): 40% as equity, 30% as debt @ 7.5 % and the remaining funds as preference share capital @ 10% of dividend.

Alternative — (iv): 30% as equity, 40% as debt @8% p.a. and the remaining funds as preference capital @ 9.5% rate of dividend.

The preference share has a par value of Rs. 100 and the applicable tax rate is 30%. You are requifed to advise which of the alternatives is better. ***(June 06, Aug. 05, Jan. 05)***

Solution :

Particulars	I Raised as equity	II 50% equity 50% debt @ 8%	III 40% equity, 30% debt <S> 7.5% 30% preference share @10%	IV 30% equity, 40% debt 98% 30% preference capital 9,9.5 %
EBIT (–) Interest on debt	9,00,000	9,00,000 1,44,000	9,00,000 81,000	9,00,000 1,15,200
EBT/PBT	9,00,000	7,56,000	8,19,000	7,84,800
(–) Tax 30%	2,70,000	2,26,000	2,45,700	2,35,440
EAT/PAT	6,30,000	5,29,200	5,73,330	5,49,360
(–) Pref. dividend (D_p)	-	-	1,08,000	1,02,600
earnings available to equity shareholder	6,30,000	5,29,200	4,65,300	4,46,760
Number of equity shares existing	1,50,000	1,50,000	1,50,000	1,50,000
(+) new shares Total No.of equity shares	3,60,000 5,10,000	1,80,000 3,30,000	1,44,000 2,94,000	1,08,000 2,58,000
EPS. $\frac{\text{Earning available to equuity share holder}}{\text{No. of equity shares}}$	4.20	1.60	1.58	1.73

Particulars	1	II	III	IV
1. % of equity financing	100%	50%	40%	30%
	36,00,000 x 100	36,00,000 x 50	36,00,000 x 40	36,00,000 x 30
2. Amount of financing of 36,00,000	36,00,000	18,00,000	14,40,000	10,80,000
	36,00,000	18,00,000	14,40,000	10,80,000
3. No. of new shares @ share price of 10.007-	10 - 36,00,000	10 18,00,000	10 14,40,000	10 10,80,000

According to EPS the option of getting a new funds can be through raising an equity as it is giving higher returns.

Note : No of equity shares assuming per value of Rs 10,0000

Example 3. *Calculate operating leverage and financial leverage under situations A, B and C and financial plans 1, 2, and 3 respectively from the following information relating to A, B and C Ltd. Also find out the combinations of operating and financial leverage which give the highest value and least value.*

Installed capacity (units) *7,600*

Actual production and sales (units). 1,200

Selling price per unit (Rs.) *15*

Variable cost per unit (Rs.) *10*

Fixed Cost

Situation A -> Rs. 2000

Situation B -> Rs. 3000

Situation C ->• Rs. 4000

Capital Structure:

	Financial Plans		
	1 Rs.	2 Rs.	3 Rs.
Equity	5000	7500	2500
Debt	5000	2500	7500
Cost of Debt (for all plans)	12%	12%	12%

Solution :

Calculation of contribution, EBIT and EBT

Situation - A (When fixed cost Rs. 2000)

	Financial Plans		
	Plan-I Rs.	Plan - II Rs.	Plan -III Rs.
Sales	18,000	18,000	18,000
Less: Variable cost	12,000	12,000	12,000
Contribution	6,000	6,000	6,000
Less: Fixed cost	2,000	2,000	2,000
EBIT	4,000	4,000	4,000
Less: Interest \1%	600	300	900
EBT	3,400	3,700	3,100

Calculation of Operating Leverage

Operating leverage = Contribution/EBIT

PLAN 1 = 6000/4000 = 1.5

PLAN 2 = 6000/4000 = 1.5

PLAN 3 = 6000/4000 = 1.5

Calculation of Financial Leverage

Financial Leverage = EBIT/EBT

PLAN 1 = 4000/3400 = 1.18

PLAN 2 = 4000/3700 = 1.08

PLAN 3 = 4000/3100 = 1.29

Calculation of Combined Leverage

Combined leverage = Operating leverage x Financial leverage

Plan 1: 1.5 × 1.8 = 1.77

Plan 2: 1.5 × 1.08 = 1.62

Plan 3: 1.5 × 1.29 = 1.94

Situation - B (When fixed cost Rs. 2000)

	Particulars	1 Rs.	2 Rs.	3 Rs.
	Sales,	18,000	18,000	18,000
Less:	Variable cost	12,000	12,000	12,000
	Controbution	6,000	6,000	6,000
Less:	Fixed cost	3,000	3,000	3,000
	EBIT →	3,000	3,000	3,000
Less:	Interest 12%	600	300	900
	EBT	2,400	2,700	2,100

Calculation of Operating Leverage

Operating leverage = Contribution / EBIT

PLAN 1 = 6000/2000 = 3.0

PLAN 2 = 6000/2000 = 3.0

PLAN 3 = 6000/2000 = 3.0

Calculation of Financial Leverage :

Financial Leverage = EBIT/EBT

PLAN 1 = 2000/1400 = 1.25

PLAN 2 = 2000/1700 = 1.11

PLAN 3 = 2000/900 = 1.43

Calculation of Combined Leverage

Combined leverage = Operating leverage x Financial leverage

Plan 1: 2 × 1.25 = 2.5

Plan 2: 2 × 1.11 = 2.22

Plan 3: 2 × 1.43 = 2.86

Situation - C (When Fixed Cost Rs. 4000)

Particulars	Financial Plans		
	1 Rs.	2 Rs.	3 Rs.
Sales	18,000	18,000	18,000
Less: Variable cost	12,000	12,000	12,000
Contribution	6,000	6,000	6,000
Less: Fixed cost	4,000	4,000	4,000
EBIT	2,000	2,000	2,000
Less: Interest 12%	600	300	900
EBT	1,400	1,700	1,100

Calculation of Operating Leverage

Operating leverage = Contribution/EBIT

PLAN 1 = 6000/2000 = 3.0

PLAN 2 = 6000/2000 = 3.0

PLAN 3 = 6000/2000 = 3.0

Calculation of Financial Leverage

Financial Leverage = EBIT/EBT

PLAN 1 = 2000/1400 = 1.25

PLAN 2 = 2000/1700 = 1.11

PLAN 3 = 200012100 = 1.43

Calculation of Combined Leverage

Combined leverage = Operating leverage × Financial leverage

Plan 1 : 3 × 1.43 = 4.29

Plan2:3 × 1.18 = 3.59

Plan 3 : 3 × 2.22 = 6.66

Example 4. *The following information is available for X and Co.*

EBIT	*12, 20,000*
Profit before tax	*Rs. 4,20,000*
Fixed cost	*Rs. 700,000*

Calculate % change in EPS if the sales are expected to increase by 5%.

Solution:

Note : In order to find out the % change in EPS as a result of % change in sales, the combined average should be calculated as follows :

Calculation of Operating Leverage : Operating leverage = Contribution/ EBIT = 1920000/12,20,000

Operating leverage = 1.573

Note : Contribution = EBIT + Fixed cost

= Rs. 12,20,000 + Rs. 700,000

= Rs. 19,20,000

Calculation of Financial Leverage : Financial Leverage = EBIT/EBT = 1220000/420000 = 2.90

Calculation of Combined Leverage : Combined leverage = Operating leverage × Financial .leverage

= 1.573 × 2.90

Combined leverage = 4.56

Example 5. *The following information has been extracted from the financial records of P, Q, and R*

	P	Q	R
Variable expenses as % sales	40	75	60
Interest expenses (Rs.) Degree of operating leverage	200 4	300 6	500 5
Degree of financial leverage	3	4	2
Income tax (%)	40	40	40

Prepare income statements for P, Q and R and comment on the financial position and structure of three turn companies.

Solution: The preparation of Income statement require the following information :

1. Sales revenue
2. Variable cost
3. Fixed cost

From the ratio DFL and DOL these figures can be calculated.

1. Calculation of EBIT with given DFL and Interest

DFL = EBIT/EBT (OR) DFL = EBIT/ EBIT-I

P => 3 = EBIT/ EBIT – 200

3(EBIT – 200) = EBIT

3EBIT – 600 = EBIT

2EBIT = 600

EBIT = 300

Q => 4 = EBIT /EBIT -300

4(EBIT – 300) = EBIT

4EBIT – 1200 = EBIT

3EBIT = 1200

EBIT = 400

Q => 2 = EBIT / EBIT – 500

2(EBIT – 500) = EBIT

2EBIT – 1000 = EBIT

EBIT = 1000

2. Calculation of sales with given DOL and EB1T.

$$DOL = \frac{\text{Sales} - \text{variable cost}}{\text{EBIT}}$$

P=> 4 = X – 0.4X/ 300

1200 = 0.6X

X = 2,000

Q=.> 6 = X – 0.75 / 400

2400 = 0.25X

X=2400/0.25

X= 9600

R=>5 = X-0.6 / 100

5000 = 0.4 X

X = 5000/ 0.4

X = 12500

Income statement *P*, *Q* and *R* :

Particulars	P Rs.	Q Rs.	R Rs.
Sales	2,000	9,600	12,500
Less : Variable cost	8,00	7,200	7,800
Contribution	1,200	2,400	
Less : Fixed cost	900	2,000	
EBIT →	300	400	
Less : interest	600	300	500
PBT	100	100	500
Less : Tax® 40%	40	40	200
PAT	60	60	300

Example 6. Determine the EPS of a textile company which has EBIT of Rs. 1,60,000. Its capital structure consists of the following securities.

10 % Debentures Rs. 500,000 12 % Preference share Rs. 700,000 Equality shares of Rs. 100 each Rs. 400,000 The company is in the 55% tax bracket.

1. *Determine the firm EPS.*
2. *Determine the percentage change in EPS associated with 30%. Increase and 30% decrease in EBIT.*
3. Determine the degree of the financial leverage.

Solution:

		Particulars Rs.	Normal Increase Rs.	30% Decrease Rs.
	EBIT	160,000	2,08,000	1,12,000
Less:	Interest 10%	50,000	50,000	50,000
	Earning before tax (EBT)	1,10,000	1,58,000	62,000
Less:	Tax ® 55 %	60,500	86,900	34,100
	Earning before tax (EAT)	49,500	71,100	27,900
Less:	Preference dividend (12SK)	12,000	12,000	12,000
	Earnings available to equity Share holders	37,500	59,100	15,900

1. Calculation of Earning Per Share (EPS)

EPS = Earnings available to share holder / No of equity shares

Normal -> 37500/ 4000 = 9.375

30% Increase = 59100/4000 = 14.775

30% Decrease = 15900/ 4000 = 3.975

2. Calculation of Percentage change in EPS

(a)If EBIT Increased by 30% thin change in EPS = 5.4

i.e., (14.775-9.375) = 5.4

for 9.375 — 5.4

for 100% — ?

100 × 5.4/ 9.375 = 57.6%

(b) If EBIT Decreased by 30% than change in EPS = 5.4

for 9.375 — 5.4

for 100% — ?

100 × 5.4/9.375 = 57.6 %

3. Calculation of Financial Leverage

Financial Leverage = EBIT/ EBT = 160000/110000

***Example* 7.** *The financial manager of a company has formulated four alternative financial* plans to *finance* Rs. 3,00,000 *required to implement its expansion programme. You are required to determine the indifferent point for each financial plan assuming 50% corporate tax rate and the face value of equity share Rs. 10 each.*

Alternative 1 : Either equity capital of Rs. 3,00,000 (Or) Rs. 1,50,000, 10% debentures and Rs. 1,50,000 equity.

Alternative 2 : Either equity capital of Rs. 3,00,000 (Or) 13% preference capital of Rs, 1,00,000 and Rs. 2,00,000 equity share capital.

Alternative 3 : Either equity capital of Rs. 3,00,000 (Or) 13% preference capital of Rs. 1,00,000 subject to divided tax of 10 per cent Rs. 1,00,000, 10% debentures and Rs. 10,000 equity.

Alternative 4 : Either equity share capital Rs. 2,00,000 and 10% debentures of Rs. 1,00,000 (Or) 13% preference capital of Rs. 1,00,000 (Or) 13% preference capital of Rs. 1,00,000, 10% debentures of Rs. 80,000 and Rs. 1,20,000 equity.

Solution:

Calculation of Indifference Point

Let EB1T be X

***Alternative 1* : (Equity Vs Equity and Debentures)**

(X–1) (1–T)–P/N1 = X–1 (1–T) – P/N2

X–0 (1–0.5)–0/30000 = (X–15000) (1 – 0.5) – 0/15000

(X–0.5X) = 2 (X–15,000) (0.5)

0.5 X = 2 (0.5 X–7,500)

0.5 X = IX–15,000

IX–0.5 X = 15,000

0.5 X = 15,000

X= 15000/0.5

X = Rs. 30000

	PLAN-1 Rs.	PLAN-2 Rs.
	30,000	30,000
	—	15,000
	30,000	15,000

Calculation of ea

EPS = Earnings available to Equity share
equity shares

Plan 1 : 15000/30000 = 0.50

Plan 2 : 7500/15000 = –0.50

***Alternative 2 :* [Equity vs Equity and Preference Share]**

(X–I)(1–T) – 0/n1 = (X–I) (1–T)–0/N2

(X–0)(1–0.5)–0/30000 = (X–0)(1–0.5)–13000 /20000

2 (0.5 X) =3 (0.5X)–13,000

IX = 1.5 X - 39,000

1.5X–X = 39,000

0.5X = 39,000

X = Rs. 78,000

	PLAN-1 Rs.	PLAN-2 Rs.
EBIT	78,000	78,000
Less : Interest	—	1
EBT	78,000	78,000
Less: Tax@ 50%	39,000	39,000
EAT	39,000	39,000
Less : Preference dividend	—	13,000
Earnings available to equity share holders	39,000	26,000

Calculation of earning per share :

EPS = Earnings available to Equity share holder / No of equity shares

Plan 1 : 39000/30000 = 1.30

Plan 2 : 26000/20000 = –1.30

Alternative 3 : **[Equity Vs [illegible] Debentures]**

1.5X–0.5X = 57,900

X = 57,900

	PLAN-1 Rs.	PLAN -2 Rs.
EBIT	57,900	57,900
Less : Interest		10,000
EBT	57,900	47,900
Less : Tax @ 50%	28,950	23,950
EAT	28,950	23,950
Less : Preference dividend		14,300
Earnings available to equity share holders	28,950	9,650

Calculation of earning per share

Earnings available to equity share holders

FPS

Number of equity shares

Rs. 28,950 Plan No 1–30,000 Rs. 965

Rs. 9,650 Plan No. 2 –0.965

Alternative 4 : **[Equity Debentures Vs Equity, Preference and Debentures]**

(X–/)(l–t)–P_P	(X–/)(l–t)–D_P
nj	= n_2
(X–10,000) (1–0.5)-0	(X–8,000) (1–0.5)–13,000
20,000 =	12,000
(X–10.000) (0.5)	(X–8,000)(0.5)–13,000
20,000 =	12,000
0.5X–5000	0.5X–4000–13,000
10	6
3X–30,000 *	5X–40,000–130,000
3X- 30,000 =	5X–170,000
5X–3X	170,000–30,000
2X *	140,000
V	1,40,000
X = 2	
X *	Rs. 70,000

Particulars	PLAN-1 Rs.	PLAN-2 Rs.
EBIT *Less* : Interest	70,000 10,000	70,000 8,000
EBT *Less* : Tax @ 50%	60,000 30,000	62,000 31,000
EAT *Less* : Preference dividend	30,000	31,000 13,000
Earnings available to equity share holders	30,000	18,000

Calculation of Earning Per Share

pp_ _ Earnings *available to equity share holders Number of equity shares*

Rs. 30,000 Plan No. 1 = 20,000 = 1.5

Rs. 18,000 Plan No. 2 = 12,000 = 1.5

COST OF CAPITAL

Introduction

Cost of capital is a central concept in financial management It is used for evaluating investment projects, for determining the capital structure, for assessing leasing proposals etc.

Capital, like any other factor of production has a cost.

For the purpose of capital budgeting decisions, benefits from undertaking a proposed project are evaluated on an after-tax basis. In fact, only the cost of debt requires tax adjustment as interest paid on debt is deductible expense from the point of view of determining taxable income whereas dividends paid either to preference shareholders or to equity holders are not eligible items as a source of deduction to determine taxable income.

To sum up, it may be said that cost of capital *(k)* consists of the following three components :

1. The riskless cost of financing *rj.*
2. The business risk premium, *b* and
3. The financial risk premium, *f*

In other words, $k = rf + b + f$

Significance of the Cost of Capital

It is a concept of vital importance in the financial decision making. It is useful as a standard for :

(*i*) Evaluating investment decisions;

(*ii*) Designing a firms debt policy; and

(*iii*) Appraising the financial performance of top management.

(i) Investment Evaluation: The primary purpose of measuring the cost of capital is its use as a financial standard for evaluating the investment projects.

The cost of capital is the minimum required rate of return on the investment project that keeps the present wealth of shareholders unchanged. Thus, the cost of capital represents a financial standard for allocating the firm's funds, supplied by owners and creditors, to the various investment projects in the most efficient manner.

(ii) Designing bebt Policy: The debt policy of a firm is significantly influenced by the cost consideration. In designing the financing policy, that is, the proportion of debt and equity in the capital structure, the firm aims at minimizing the overall cost of capital.

The cost of capital is useful in deciding about the methods of financing like comparison of cost in choosing between leasing and borrowing.

(iii) Performance Appraisal: The cost of capital framework can be used to evaluate the financial performance of top management. Such an evaluation will involve a comparison of actual profitabilities of the investment projects undertaken by the firm with the projected overall cost of capital, and the appraisal of the actual costs incurred by management in raising the required funds. The cost of capital also plays a useful role in dividend decision and investment in current assets.

Types of Cost of Capital

The following are the different types of cost of capital.

1. Opportunity Cost of Capital : Decision making is the process of choosing among alternatives. In investment decisions, best alternative has to be chosen from innumerable competing investment opportunities. Each investment opportunity reflects equivalent risk as one has to forego the opportunity of investing in other alternative thus incurring an opportunity cost equal to the return on the foregone investment opportunity.

The opportunity cost is the rate of return foregone on the next best alternative investment opportunity of comparable risk. And is technically referred as implicit cost of capital.

2. Explicit and Implicit Cost : The cost of capital can be either explicit or implicit. The distinction between explicit and implicit costs is important from the point of view of the computation of the cost of capital.

The explicit cost of any source is the discount rate that equates the present value of the cash inflows that are incremental to the taking of the financing opportunity with the present value of its incremental cash outflows.

When firms raise funds from different sources, there is a series of cash flows. Initially, there is cash inflow to extent of the amount raised. This is followed by a series of cash outflows in respect of interest payments, repayment of principal, or payment of dividends.

The general formula for the explicit cost of capital of any source of raising finance would be as follows :

$$CI_0 = \sum_{t=1}^{n} \frac{CO^t}{(1+C)^t}$$

Where $C/_0$ * initial cash inflow, that is, net cash proceeds received by the firm from the capital source at time O COi + *CO2* ... + $C0_n$ = cash outflows at times 1, 2, ..n, that is, cash payment from the firm to the capital source.

The explicit cost of capital is the *'rate of return of the cash flows of the financing opportunity'*. In other words, it is the internal rate of return that the firm pays to produce financing.

The explicit cost of capital is concerned with incremental cash flows that result directly from raising funds.

Retained earnings used in the firm involve no future cash flows to, or from the firm. The retained earnings are undistributed profit of the company belonging to the shareholders. Given the ultimate objective of the firm to maximize the wealth of shareholders, the cost of retained earning would be equivalent to the opportunity cost of earning by investing elsewhere by the shareholders themselves or by the company itself. Opportunity cost are technically referred to as implicit cost of capital. The implicit cost of capital of funds raised and invested by the firm may, therefore, be defined as *'the rate of return associated with the best investment opportunity for the firm and its shareholders that would be foregone, if the projects presently under consideration by the firm were accepted.* The cost of retained earnings is an opportunity cost of implicit capital cost, in the sense that it is the rate of return at which the shareholders could have invested these funds had they been distributed to them. The explicit costs arises when funds are raised, whereas the implicit costs arise when funds are used.

3. Specific Cost of Capital: The cost of capital on each source of capital is known as *component or specific cost of capital.*

4. Weighted Average Cost of Capital (WACC): The component costs are combined according to the weight of each component capital to obtain the average cost of capital. Thus the overall cost is also called as the weighted average cost of capital.

Component Costs and Computation

The cost of capital on each source of capital i.e., debt, preference capital, equity is known as *component or specific cost of capital.*

DETERMINING COMPONENT (OR) SPECIFIC COST OF CAPITAL

The following are the methods of computing the component

costs of three major sources of capital: debt, preference and equity shares. The component cost of a specific source of capital is equal to the investors required rate of return and reflects investors opportunity cost of a source of capital.

$$C_o = \sum_{t=1}^{n} \frac{CFAT_t}{(1+k)^t}$$

Where C_0 is the capital supplied by investor in current period (O) representing net cash inflow to the firm and *CFAT* are returns expected by investors representing cash outflows to the firm and *k* is the investors required rate of return or cost of capital to the firm.

The investors, required rate of return should be adjusted for taxes in practice for calculating the cost of specific source of capital to the firm. In the investment analysis, net cash flows are computed on an after-tax basis, therefore, the component costs, used to determine the discount rate, should also be expressed on an after-tax basis.

1. Cost of Debt ***(k_d):*** A company may raise debt in a variety of ways. It may borrow funds from financial Institutions or public either in the form of public deposits or debentures (bonds) for a specified period of time at a certain rate of Interest, A debenture or bond may be issued at par or at a discount or premium. The contractual rate of interest forms the basis for calculating the cost of any form of debt.

(*i*) Cost of debt before taxes (issued at par redeemed at par) = *1 / Po "o*

(*ii*) Cost of debt before taxes (Issued at discount or premium redeemed at par)

= 1 + (RV–SV)n

(RV–SV)/2

(*iii*) After tax cost of debt = $k_d\,(1 - t)$ where

i = interest

RV = Redeemable value

$P_0 = SV$ = Net sale proceeds i.e., issue price after flotation costs i.e., $P_0\,(1\text{–}f)$

n = Years to maturity

t = corporate tax rate.

2. Cost of Preference Capital *(k_p)* : Preference capital carries a fixed rate of dividend and is redeemable in nature. The obligation of a company towards its preference shareholders are not as firm as those towards its debenture holders. Assuming that preference dividend will be paid regularly and preference capital will be redeemed as per the original intent.

Preference stock is considered much like a bond with fixed commitments. However, preference dividend, unlike debt interest, is not a tax - deductible expense.

The-cost of preference capital is a function of the dividend expected by investors.

(a) Irredeemable preference share (k_p) = D/Po

(b) Redeemable preference share = $\dfrac{D + \dfrac{RV - SV}{n}}{\dfrac{RV + SV}{2}}$

D = Dividend

RV = Redeemable value

$p_o = SV$ = Net sale proceeds i.e., issue price after flotation costs i.e., $P_0\,(1\text{–F})$

n = Years to maturity

3. Cost of Equity *(k_e)* *or* External Equity : Equity finance may be obtained in two ways:

(a) Retention of earnings; and

(b) Issue of additional equity.

A firm raises equity finance by retaining earnings or issuing additional equity shares, the cost of equity is the same. The only differences is in floatation costs. There is no floatation cost for retained earnings whereas there is a flotation cost for additional equity.

Thus, the cost of equity refers to the cost of retained earnings as well as the cost of external equity.

The required rate of return is equal to a risk-free rate, *Rf*, plus a risk premium, *Rp* whereas the expected rate of return, assuming a constant growth in dividends, is equal to dividend yield, *D*1/*P*0, plus expected growth rate, *g*.

ke = Required rate of return = Expected rate of return.

$Ke = Rf + Rp = DI/Po + $ g where $D_1 = D_0\,(1 + g)$

Therefore, the cost of equity (*kE* can be estimated either as $Rf + Rp$ or $DI/Po + g$

A popular approach to estimating the cost of equity is CAPM approach. According to this approach company's equity is

$$Ke \;=\; Rf + \text{Beta}\,(rm - rp)$$

4. Cost of Retained Earnings (k_r) : The cost of retained earnings must be considered as the opportunity cost of the foregone dividends. From the point of view of equity shareholders, any earning retained by the firm could have been profitably invested by the equity shareholders themselves, had these been distributed to them. Thus, there is an opportunity cost involved in the firms retaining the earnings and an estimation of this cost can be taken up as a measure of cost of capital of retained earnings, k_r.

The cost of retained earnings, is often taken as equal to the cost of equity share capital, k_e, since the retained earnings are viewed as the fresh subscription to the equity share capital. ∴ So, $k_r = k_e\,(1-f)\,(1-t)$ where t is shareholders tax rate.

The computation of cost of equity under different approach is as follows :

1.(CAPM approach)

$$k_e = R_f + p\,(R_m - R_f)$$

2. (Dividend approach)

(a) k_e (no growth from) – D/Po

(b) k_e (Constant growth) – $D1/Po + g$ where $D1 = D_0 (1 + g)$

Where PO= Current market price of stock after flotation costs i.e. $P_0\,(1–f)$.

DI = Dividend expected to be paid at the end of year 1

g - Constant growth rate

3. Earnings Approach

K_e (Earnings Approach) = $EPS1/Po$

EPS1 is the expected earnings per share and the expected earnings–price ratio may be used as a measure of the cost of equity for expansion, A firm is said to be expanding, if the investment opportunities available to it are expected to earn a rate of return equal to cost of equity.

WACC Computation and Assigning Weight!

1. Weighted Average Cost of Capital (WACC) Computation : The component costs are combined according to the weight of each component capital to obtain the average cost of capital. Thus, the overall cost is also called the weighted average cost of capital.

A company's cost of capital is the weighted average cost of various sources of finance used by It, viz., equity, preference, and debt.

Suppose that a company uses equity, preference, and debt In the following proportions: 50, 10, and 40. If the component costs of equity, preference, and debt are 16 per cent, 12 per cent, and 8 per cent respectively, the weighted average cost of capital *(WACC)* will be :

W&CC = (Proportion of equity) {Cost of equity) + (Proportion of preference) (Cost of preference) + {proportion of debt) (Cost of debt).

= (0.5)(16) + (0.10)(12) + (0.4)(8) – 12.4 per cent.

The weighted average cost of capital may be expressed as follows :

$WACC = W_e k_e + W_p k_p + W_d r_d (1-t) + W_r k_r$ where

W = proportion (or) weighted of equity,

k = Cost of equity, preference and preference debt referred earnings debts and retained earnings.

t = Corporate tax rate.

Important consideration while calculating average cost of capital (or) WACC.

1. For the sake of simplicity, only three types of capital equity, non convertible and non callable preference capital and debt are considered.
2. Debt includes long term and short term debt.
3. Non-interest bearing liabilities. Such as trade creditors, are not included in the calculation of the weighted average cost of capital.

Rationale : The rationale for using WACC as hurdle rate in capital budgeting is, if a firms rate of return on its investment exceeds its cost of capital, equity shareholders are benefited.

2. Assignment of Weights: In order to calculate the WACC, there must be a system of assigning weights to different specific cost of capital. The following considerations are important while assigning weights to specific cost of capital to findout the WACC.

Historical, Marginal and Target Weights : The WACC is found by weighing the specific cost of capital for each type of financing by its proportion in the overall capital structure. The weights which may be assigned and used to find out the WACC may be as follows :

(a) Historical or Existing Weights : Historical or existing weights are the weights based on the actual or existing proportions of different sources In the overall capital structure. Such weighing system is based on the actual proportions at the time when the WACC is being calculated. In other words, the weighing system is the proportions in which the funds have already been raised by the firm.

(b) *Marginal Weights* **:** *The proportions in which the firm wants to raise additional* funds from different sources to finance the investment proposals are known as marginal weights. So, in case of marginal weights, the firm calculates the actual WACC *of* the incremental funds. Theoretically, the system of marginal weights is good enough as the return from investment will be compared with the actual cost of funds.

(c) *Target Weights* **:** The target weights refer to the proportion in which the firm plans to raise the funds from various sources in the long run. In other words, the *target weights system reflects the desired long-term financial plans or capital* structure of a firm.

3. Book Value Versus Market Value Weights : The weights to be used for calculations of WACC can either be based on the book value or the market value of the funds raised from different sources.

(a) *Book* Value Weights : The weights are said to be book value weights if the proportions of different sources are ascertained on the basis of the face values i.e., the accounting values. The book value weights can be easily calculated by taking the relevant information from the capital structure as given in the balance sheet of the firm.

(b) *Market Value Weights* : The weights may also be calculated on the basis of the market value of different sources i.e., the proportion of each source at its market value. In order to calculate the market value weights, the firm has to find out the current market price of the securities in each categories.

4. WACC Vs WMCC : The commonly known cost in the context of investment and financing decisions is the weighted average cost of capital (WACC).

The weighted average cost of incremental capital should be used in capital expenditure decisions. The weighted average cost of new, or incremental, capital is known as *marginal cost of capital*

Weighted average cost of total hew funds is called as *weighted average cost of capital (WACC)* and weighted average cost of additional new capital is called *weighted marginal cost of capital (WMCC).*

Cost of Equity and CAPM Approaches

(A) k_c and CAPM Approach

The firm's weighted average cost of capital reflects the average risk of all projects, therefore, it can be used for investment evaluation only when the risk of the projects is equal to the firm's average risk. The firm's WACC should be adjusted for the risk characteristics of the project :

Project's cost of capital = WACC + Risk adjustment factor

The risk adjustment factor can be determined by the decision maker on the basis of his experience and judgement.

The capital asset pricing model can be used to formally adjust for risk in the calculation of the cost of equity. A risky security such as company's share requires a rate of return equal to :

Required rate of return = Risk free rate + risk premium

The risk of the share can be measured by its beta, which is given by the following equation.

$Beta\ (B) = cov_{im/sd}^{2}$

Where Bj is the beta of share

COV_{im} the covariance between the returns of the share and the market portfolio and sd^2 the variance of the market portfolio. In practice, beta can also be calculated by regressing the returns of the share with the market returns, (i.e., the change in the share price index).

The required rate of return on a share is the cost of equity from a company's point of view. Thus, the cost of equity is given by the following formula :

$$Ke = Rf + (R_m - R_f)Bj$$

The difference between the market return R_m and the risk free rate fly is the risk-premium. The cost of equity will increase with beta.

(B) Cost of Equity : CAPM Vs Dividend Growth Model

Dividend Growth approach assumes that dividend per share will grow at a constant rate and expected dividend growth rate should be less than cost of equity to arrive at simple growth formula. These assumptions imply that the dividend growth approach is not applicable to those companies which do not pay any dividends or whose dividend per share grow at a higher rate than k_e or whose dividend policies are highly volatile. Also, dividend growth approach fails to deal with risk.

CAPM has a wider application though it is based on restrictive assumptions as all variables in CAPM are market determined. The value of beta is determined in an objective manner by using sound statistical methods. But the problem with the use of beta is, it is highly volatile.

ILLUSTRATIONS

Example 1. *A company decides to sell a new issue of 7-year 15% bonds of Rs. 100 each at par. Find out the before tax cost of debt. If tax rate is 30%, find out after tax cost of debt.*

Solution : (*a*) Kd (Before Tax) = I/Po = 15/ 100 = 15%

k_d (after tax) = k_d (1–t) = 15(1–0.3) = 10.5%

(b) If the above bond is sold at a discount of 94 /-

$$\text{before tax kd} = \frac{1+(RV–SV)n}{(RV–SV)/2} = \frac{15+1/7(100-94)}{½(100+94)}$$

$$= \frac{15.86}{97} = 16.4\%$$

After tax *kd* = 0.164(1–0.3) = 11.48%

(c) If the above bond is sold at discount for a net price of 97.75 and redeemed at 5% premium.

$$k_d \text{ (before tax)} = \frac{1+(RV-SV)n}{(RV-SV)/2}$$

$$= \frac{15+1/7(105-97.75)}{½(105+97.75)} = 15.8\%$$

2 *kd* (aftertax) = 0.158(1–0.3) = 11.06%.

Example 2. *The current market price of a company's share is Rs. 90 and the expected dividend per share next year is Rs. 4.50. If the dividends are expected to grow at a constant rate of 8 per cent, the shareholder's required rate of return is:*

Solution : *Ke* = *D* / *Po* + *g*

Ke = Rs 4.50 / 90 + 0.08 = 0.05 + 0.08 = 0.13 or 13%

If the company intends to retain earnings, it should atleast earn a return of 13 per cent on retained earnings to keep the current market price unchanged.

The share of a company is currently selling for Rs. 100. It wants to finance its capital expenditures of Rs. 1,00,000 either by retaining earnings or selling new shares. If the company sells new shares, the issue price will be Rs. 95. The dividend per share next year is Rs. 4.75 and it is expected to grow at 6 per cent. Calculate

(i) The cost of internal equity (retained earnings), and

(ii) The cost of external equity (new issue of shares).

Answer : The cost of internal equity :

Ke = *Rs* 4.75/100 + 0.06 = 0.0475 + 0.06 = 0.1075 Or 10.75%

The cost of external equity :

Ke = 4.75/95 + 0.06 = 0.05+0.06 = 0.11 or 11%.

It is obvious that the cost of external equity is greater than the cost of internal equity because of the under pricing {cost of external equity = 11% > cost of internal equity = 10.75%).

Assuming that a firm pays tax at a 50% rate, compute after tax cost of capital in the following cases :

(i) A 8.5 per cent preference share sold at par.

(ii) A perpetual bond sold at par, rate of interest being 7 per cent.

(iii) A ten-year, 8 per cent, Rs. 1000 par bond sold at Rs. 950 less 4-per cent underwriting commission.

(iv) A preference share sold at Rs. 100 with a 9 'per cent dividend and a redemption price of Rs. 110 if the company redeems it in five years.

(v) An ordinary share selling at a current market price of Rs. 120, and paying a current dividend of Rs. 9 per share which is expected to grow at a rate of 8 per cent.

(vi) An ordinary share of a company which engages no external financing is selling for Rs. 50. The earnings per share are Rs. 7.50 of which sixty per cent is paid in dividends. The company reinvests retained earnings at a rate of 10 per cent.

Solution : (*i*) The after-tax cost of the preference issue will be 8.5 per cent,

(*ii*) The after-tax cost of bond is :

$kd\ (1-t) = 0.07\ (1-0.5) = 0.035$ or 3.5%

(*iii*) The after-tax cost of bond is :

$$= \frac{1+(RV-SV)/n(1-t)}{(RV-SV)/2} = \frac{80+1/10(1000-950)(1-0.5)}{½(1000+950)}$$

$$= 42.50/975 = 0.0436 \text{ or } 4.36\%$$

$$kp = \frac{D+(RV–SV)/n}{(RV–SV)/2} = \frac{9+(110-100)/5}{½(110+100)}$$

By trial and error, we find k_p = 0.105 or 10.5%.

(*v*) *ke* = *D1* / *Po* + *g* = *Rs.* 9 (1.08)/120 + 0.08

= *Rs. 9.72* / *120 + 0.08*

0.081 + 0.08 = 0.161 or 16.1%

Where *DI* = D_0 (1 + *g*)

D1 = 9 (1 + 0.08) = 9 (1–0.8)

(*vi*) *Po* = *EPS(l–b)* / *ke–br*

ke = *EPS (1–b)* / *Po* + *br* = 7.50 (1–0.50)/50 + 0.10 * 0.40

Rs 4.50/50 + 0.04 = 0.09 + 0.04 = 0.13 or 13 per cent

Example 5. *The company has the following capital structure at 31 March, 1998 which is considered to be optimum.*

	Rs.
14% Debentures	*3,00,000*
11 % Preference	*1,00,000*
Equity (1,00,000 shares)	*16,00,000*
	20,00,000

The company's share has a current market price of Rs. 23.60 per share. The expected dividend per share next year is 50 per cent of the 1998 EPS. The following are the earnings per share figure for the company during the preceding ten years. The past trends are expected to continue.

Years	ESPRs	Year	EPSRs
1998	1.00	1994	1.61
1990	1.10	1995	1.77
1991	1.21	1996	1.95
1992 .	1.33	1997	2.15
1993	1.46	1998	2.36

The company can issue 16 per cent new debentures. The

company's debenture is currently selling at Rs. 96. The new preference issue can be sold at a net price of Rs. 9.20, paying a dividend of Rs. 1.1 per share. The company's marginal tax rate is 50 per cent.

Calculate the after tax cost (i) of new debt, (ii) of new preference capital and (Hi) of ordinary equity, assuming new equity comqs from retained earnings.

Solution : The existing capital structure of the firm is assumed to be optimum. Thus, the optimum proportions are :

Type of Capital	Amount (Rs.)	Proportions
14% Debentures	3,00,000	0.15
11 % Preference	1,00,000	0.05
Equity -"	16,00,000	0.80
	20,00,000	1.00

(a) (i) After tax cost of debt (current)

KD = Rs.16/96 = 0.1667

k_d (1–T) = (1–0.5) (0.1667) = 0.0833

Note : The above formula is used since the maturity period of the debentures is not given

(ii) After tax cost of preference capital (current) :

KP = Rs.1.1 / 9.20 = 0.12

Note : Preference shares are assumed to be irredeemable,

(iii) After tax cost of retained earnings :

Ke = div1 / po + g = 1.18/23.60 + 0.10 = 0.05 + 0.10 = 0.15

DIV1 = 50% of 1998 EPS = 50% of Rs. 2.36 = Rs. 1.18.

Calculation of *g* :

It can be observed from the best trends of EPS that it is growing at an annual compound rate of 10 per cent. For example $E_t = EO\ (1 + g)^t$ = Rs. 2.36 = Re 1 $(1 + g)^9$. Using Table *A*, we find that the present value factor of 2.36 at the end of 9th year is obtained when the interest rate is 10 percent. The growth rate is, therefore, 10 per cent.

Type of Capital (D	Proportion	Specific Cost	Product (2) x (3) *
1	2	3	4
Debt.	0.15	0.0833	0.0125
Preference	0.05	0.1200	0.0060
Equity	0.80	0.1500	0.1200
Marginal cost of capital			*0.1385* or 13. 85 %

Example 6. *XVZ Limited is in a tax bracket of 33%. For the following specific instruments, you are required to find the after-tax cost of capital:*

(i) The face value of perpetual bond is Rs. 1,000. It carries a coupon of 9%. Find the post-tax cost of debt.

(ii) The par value of a bond is Rs. 1,000. The coupon is 10% and the company issued it at Rs. 945. The floatation cost incurred is 3% and the bond's life is 8 years. Find the after-tax cost of debt.

(iii) A preference share b sold for Rs. 100 today and is-to be redeemed after four years at Rs. 118. The preference dividend is 11%. Find the cost of preference for the company.

(iv) The equity shares of the company are currently traded at Rs. 126 per share. The latest dividend paid was Rs. 11 per share. If the dividend of the company are expected to grow at 7.5 per cent, what would be the cost of equity for the firm ? ***(June 2005)***

Solution: (*i*) k_d (after tax) = 0.09(1–0.33) = 6.03%

(*ii*) *kd* (before tax) = = 1 + *(RV–SV) / n* = 100 + 1/8(1000-915) = 110.625/957.5 = 11.55

SV = Issue price–flotation costs

= 945–1000 x 3%

= 945–30 = 915

k_d (after tax) = 0.1155(1–0.33) = 7.74%

(*iii*) kp = *D* + *(RV–SV) / n* = 11 + 1/4(118 – 100) = 15.5/109 = 14.22% (RS–SV)/2 ½ (118+100)

***Example 7.** A company has the following capital structure.*

	Rs.
12% Debentures.	26,00,000
8 % Preference	*20,000*
Share Premium	*1,00,000*
Equity (1,00,000 shares)	25,00,000

The *equity stock is currently selling at Rs. 60 per share and is expected to get the dividend will of 4.00. Stockholders anticipate that the equity stock dividend grow at a rate of 6% per annum in the near future. The company has a tax rate of 60%. From the above information you are required to calculate the cost of capital of the company.* ***(June 2007)***

Solution : *Kd* = 0.12 (1 -0.6) = 4.8%

$k_p = 8\%$

Ke = D1/Po + g = Do (1+*g*)/*Po* + *g* = 4 (1.06)/60 + 0.06 = 13.07%

Cost of capital of the company (k_0) is given by . . = $wd\ k_d + w_p\ k_p + w_e k_e$

= 0.498 x 0.048 + 0.003 x 0.008 + 0.479 x 0.1307 = 0.024 + 0.00024 + 0.063 = 0.087 = 8.7%.

***Example 8.** Following are the details regarding the capital structure of a company:*

Type of Capital	Book Value Rs.	Market Value Rs.	Specific Cost Rs.
Debentures	40,000	38,000	5%
Preference Capital	10,000	11,000	8%
Equity Capital	60,000	90,000	13%
Retained earnings	20,000	30,000	9%

You are required to calculate the weighted average cost of capital using (i) book values (ii) market values.

(Ian 07, Oct. 02)

Solution :

(*i*) Computation of weighted average cost of capital (Basis : Books values)

Source	Amount	Weight	After tax cost of capital	Weighted cost of capital (Rs.) 5 = (3) x (4)
1	2	3	4	5
Debentures	40,000	0.3076	5%	1.53%
Preference capital	10,000	0.0769	8%	0.61%
Equity capital	60,000	0.4615	13%	5.99%
Retained Earnings	20,000	0.1538	9%	1.38%
Weighted average cost of capital (*ko*)				9.51%

What type of relationship you observe between risk(Bj) and the cost of equity for the firm.

Show the relationship graphically and present your observations (Aug. 04)

Solution : We know

Ke = Rf + B(Rm – Rf)

When $BJ = 0.43\ k_e = 0.09 + 0.43(0.2–0.09)$
$= 13.73\%–$

When $Bj = 0.87\ k_e = 0.09 + 0.87\ (0.2–0.09)$
$= 18.57\ \%$

When $Bj = 1.09\ k_e = 0.09 + 1.09\ (0.2–0.09)$
$= 20.99\ \%$

When $Bj = 1.48\ k_e = 0.09 + 1.48\ (0.2–0.09)$
$= 25.28\ \%$

When $Bj = 1.88\ k_e = 0.09 + 1.88(0.2–0.09)$
$= 29.68\%$

With the increase in *Bj* there is also increase in k_e. The graphical presentation of the above would give the following figure which is similar to SML.

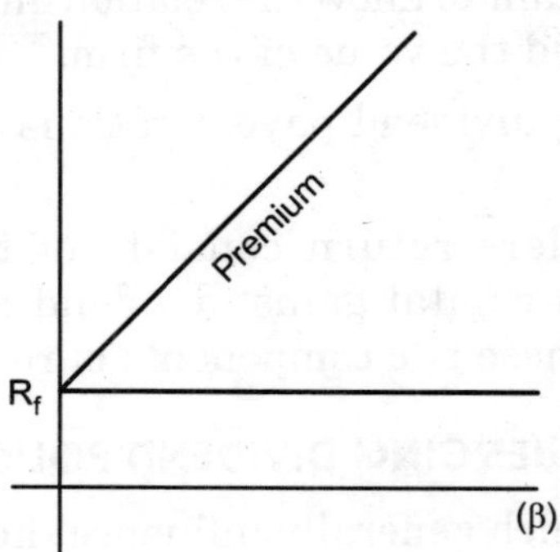

DIVIDEND DECISIONS

Dividend Policy

Introduction

The dividend policy of a firm determines what proportion of earnings is paid to shareholders by the way of dividends and what proportion is retained in the firm for reinvestment. A firm dividend payout will intern depend on how earnings are measured.

Aspects of Dividend Policy : A firm's dividend policy has the effect of dividing its net earnings into two parts: retained earnings and dividends. The retained earnings provide funds to finance the firm's long-term growth. It is the most significant source of financing a firm's investments in practice.

Dividends are paid in cash. Thus, the distribution of earnings uses the available cash of the firm. A firm which intends to pay dividends and also needs funds to finance its investment opportunities will have to use external sources of financing, such as the issue of debt or equity. Dividend policy of the firm, thus, has its effect on both the long-term financing and the wealth of shareholders.

Issues in Dividend Policy

(a) The principal objectives of financial management is to maximize the wealth of the shareholders and hence it is important to know the relationship between dividend policy and the value of the firm.

(b) Deciding dividend payout ratio is another important aspect.

Shareholders return consists of two components : dividends and capital gains, dividend policy has a direct influence on these two components of returns.

FACTORS INFLUENCING DIVIDEND POLICY

The factors which generally influence the dividend policy of the firm are as follows:

(a) ***Shareholders Expectations :*** The directors should give due importance to the expectations of shareholders in the matter of dividend decision. Shareholder's preference for dividends or capital gains may depend on their economic status and the effect of tax on dividends and capital gains.

(b) ***Institutional Investors*** : Purchase large blocks of shares to hold them for relatively long periods of time. Institutional investors, are not connected with profitable investments. Most institutional investors avoid speculative issues, seek diversification in their investment portfolio and favour a policy of regular cash dividend payments.

(c) ***Policy Consideration :*** The dividend policy, once established, should be continued as long as it does not interfere with the financing needs of the company. A definite dividend policy, followed for a long period in the past, attracts those investors who consider the dividend policy in accord with their investment requirements. Thus an established dividend policy should be changed slowly only after analyzing its probable effects on the existing shareholders.

Dimension of Dividend Policy

The two important dimensions of a firms dividend policy are:

(1) Determination of dividend payout ratio, (*i*) Payout Ratio (*ii*) Stability of dividends :

The consideration relevant for determining the dividend payout ratio are described below:

1. Firms which have substantial investment opportunities keep the dividend payout ratio low and firms which have limited investment opportunities keep the dividend payout high.
2. A firm may not be able to distribute more earnings as dividend because of insufficient liquidity.
3. A firm which has easy access to external financing may pay high dividend. A firm which has difficulty on raising finances distribute lower dividends.
4. When equity shareholders have greater interest in current dividends, the firm may pay high dividend. If they have greater interest in long-term gain, the firm may pay low dividend.
5. It external financing leads to no dilution in control, the firm may pay high dividend else the firm may pay low dividend.
6. Dividend income is tax exempt for investor while the firm has to pay tax for distributing dividends.

(*ii*) **Stability of Dividends :** The year-to-year dividends may be determined mainly by one of the following guidelines:

1. *Stable Dividend Payout Ratio :* According to this policy, the percentage of earnings paid out as dividends remains constant. As a result, dividends fluctuate in line with earnings. Such policy result in transmission of the variability of earnings to dividends. Hence such a policy is rarely adopted by business firms.
2. ***Stable Dividend Per Share* :** As per this policy, the rupee level of dividends remains stable or gradually increases or decreases. Such a policy seems to be followed widely by business firms.

3. *Stable Dividend Per Share Plus Extra Dividend :* A fixed amount of dividend is paid regularly by the way of interim dividend, without default and allows a great deal of flexibility for supplementing the income of shareholders when the earnings of the company are high by the way of extra dividend.

RATIONALE FOR DIVIDEND STABILITY

- Many individual investors depend on dividend income to meet a portion of their living expenses. Sharp changes in dividend income may entail selling of shares. These are avoided if the dividend stream is stable and predictable.
- The dividend decision of the firm is being to be regarded as an important means by which the management conveys information about the prospects of the firm.
- Institutional investors often view a record of steady dividend payment as a precondition before considering equity or debt investment in the firm.

Forms of Dividends

The usual practice is to pay dividends in cash. Other option is payment of the bonus shares or stock dividend.

1. Cash Dividend : Most companies pay dividends in cash. The cash account and the reserves account of a company will be reduced when the cash dividend is paid. Thus, both the total assets and the net worth of the company are reduced when the cash dividend is distributed.

2. Bonus Shares (Stock Dividend) : An issue of bonus share represents a distribution of shares in addition to the cash dividend to the existing shareholders. This has the effect of increasing the number of outstanding shares of the company proportionately.

(*i*) Bonus shares can be issued only out of free reserves built out of profits,

(*ii*) The shareholder proportional ownership remain unchanged.

(*iii*) The book value per share, the earnings per share, and the market price per share decrease as the number of share increase.

Reasons for Issuing Bonus Shares : The following are the important reasons for issue of bonus shares.

- The bonus issue tends to bring the market price per share within a more popular range.
- It increases the number of outstanding shares. This promotes more active trading.
- The share capital base increases and the company may achieve a more respectable size in the eyes of the investing community.
- Shareholders regard a bonus issue as a firm indication that the prospects of the company have brightened and they can reasonably look for an increase in total dividends.
- It improves the prospects of raising additional funds. In recent years many firms have issued bonus shares prior to the Issue of convertible debentures or other financing instruments.

3. Stock Split : The stock split is not a form of dividend, but its effect are similar to the effects of bonus shares. In a stock split, the par value per share is reduced or increased and the number of shares is increased or decreased proportionately.

COMPARISON BETWEEN STOCK DIVIDEND AND STOCK SPLIT

A comparison between a bonus issue and a stock split is given below :

Bonus Issue	Stock Split
The par value of the share is unchanged	The par value of the share is reduced
A part of reserves is capitalised	There is no capitalization of reserves.

The common aspects are as follows :

- The shareholder's proportional ownership remains unchanged.
- The book value per share, the earnings per share, and the market price per share decline.
- The market price per share is brought within a popular trading range.

DIVIDEND THEORIES

Relevance Models

The following are some models which assume that investment and dividend decisions are related. Two such models are the Walter and the Gordon Model.

1. Walter Model : This is a model of share valuation which supports the view that the dividend policy of the firm has a bearing on share valuation. This model is based on the following assumptions :

- The firm is an all-equity financed entity. It will rely only on retained earnings to finance its future investments. This means that the investment decision is dependent on the dividend decision.
- The rate of return on investments is constant.
- The firm has an infinite life :

Based on the above assumptions, Walter put forward the following valuation

formula:

$$P = \frac{D + (E-D)r/k}{k}$$

Where P = price per equity share

D = Dividend per share

E = Earnings per share

$(E-D)$= Retained earnings per, share

r = rate of return on investments

k = cost of capital

In Walter's model, the optimum dividend policy depends on the relationship between the firm's rate of return, r and its cost of capital, k. Walter's view on the optimum dividend-payout ratio can be summarized as follows :

(i) **Growth Firm :** Internal Rate More Than Opportunity Cost of Capital ($r > k$) Growth firms are the firms that are able to reinvest earnings at a rate (r) which is higher than the rate expected by shareholders (k). They will maximize the value per share if they follow a policy of retaining all earnings for internal investment. The market value per share increases as payout ratio declines when $r > k$.

(ii) **Normal Firms :** Internal Rate Equals Opportunity Cost of Capital ($r - k$) : For the normal firms with $r = Jc$, the dividend policy has not effect on the market value per share in Walter's model. There is no unique optimum payout ratio for a normal firm. The market price per share is not affected by the payout ratio when $r - k$.

(iii) **Declining Firms :** Internal Rate Less Than Opportunity Cost of Capital ($r > k$): The market value per share of a declining firm with $r < k$ will be maximum when it does not retain earnings at all.

Thus, in Walter's model, the dividend policy of the firm depends on the availability of investment opportunities and the relationship between the firm's internal rate of return, r and its cost of capital k. Thus waiter model implies that in case of growth firms optimal payout is not incase of declining firms optimal payout is 100% in case of normal firms.

- Retain all earnings when $r > k$.
- Distribute all earnings when $r < k$.
- Dividend (or retention) policy has no effect when $r = k$.

2. Gordon Model: Myron Gordon proposed a model of stock valuation using the dividend capitalization approach. His model is based on the following assumptions.

- Regained earnings represent the only source of financing for the firm.
- The rate of return on the firm's investment is constant.
- The cost of capital for the firm remains constant and it is greater than the growth rate.
- The firm has a perpetual life.
- Tax does not exist.

Gordon's valuation formula is

$$P = \frac{EI(1-b)}{K-br}$$

Where PO = price per share at the end of year 0

$E1$ = Earnings per share at the end of year 1

$(1–b)$ = fraction of earnings the firm distributes by way of dividends,

b = Fraction of earnings the firm ploughs back. k = rate of return required by the shareholders

r = rate of return earned on investments made by the firm,

br—growth rate of earnings and dividends.

The Basic Gordon model implies that,

- When the rate of return is greater than the discount rate ($r > k$), the price per share increases as the dividend payout ratio decreases.
- When the rate of return is equal to the discount rate ($r = k$), the price per share remains unchanged in response to variations in the dividend payout ratio.
- When the rate of return is less than the discount rate ($r < ke$), the price per share increases as the dividend payout ratio increases.

Dividends and Uncertainty : The Bird-in-the-Hand Argument: According to Gordon's model, dividend policy is irrelevant where r = *k,* when all other assumptions are held valid. But when the simplifying assumptions are modified to confirm more closely with reality, Gordon concludes that dividend policy does affect the value of a share even when r = *k.* Investors, behaving rationally, are risk-averse and, therefore, have a preference for near dividends to future dividends. This logic underlying the dividend effect on the share value is described as the bird-in-the-hand argument.

3. Lintner's Model: Most firms, in addition to maintaining a stable rupee amount of dividend, also have target payout ratios (long-run dividend payout ratio) which they aim at to avoid the necessity of reducing the dividend and to maintain progress towards the target payout ratio, firms raise their dividends per share rise. Thus, Lintner concludes that dividends represent the primary active decision variable in most situations.

According to Lintner, *dividend is a function of earnings of that year, existing dividend rate, target payout ratio and speed of adjustment.*

Lintner expressed corporate dividend behaviour in the form of the following mode:

$D_t = crEPS_t + (1\text{-}c)D\ t\text{-}1$

WhereD_t - dividend per share for year t

c = adjustment rate

r = target payout rate

EPSt - earnings per share for year t

D_{t-1} = dividend per share for year t-1

4. Miller and Modlgliani Irrelevance Model : The MM argument is based on the following assumptions :

- There is not tax advantage or disadvantage associated with dividends.

- The investment and dividend decisions of the firm are independent.
- Firms can issue stock without incurring any floatation or transaction costs to raise money for investment projects.

MM Model States' That : If a company retains earnings instead of giving it out as dividends, shareholders enjoy capital appreciation equal to the amount of earnings retained. If It distributes earnings by way of dividends instead of retaining it, the shareholders enjoy dividends equal in value to the amount by which his capital would have appreciated had the company chosen to retain its earnings. Hence, the division of earnings between dividends and retained earnings is irrelevant from the point of view of the shareholders.

1. Market price per share $P0 = \dfrac{DP_1}{1+k}$
2. Total amount of new equity shares issued $mP1 = I-(X-nDt)$
3. Value of outstanding equity shares $nPo = 1/1+k(nD1+(n+m)P1-mp1)$

Substituting 2 in 3 we get

$$nP_0 = 1/1+k\ [(n+m)P_1-I+X]$$

Where DI = DPS *at ti*

$P1$ = Current market price of share

n = Number of existing equity shares.

m = Number of new equity shares to be issued.

nPo ~ Total market value of existing equity shares at time 0.

$nD1$ = Total dividends payable on existing equity shares outstanding attime 0.

$(n + m)\ PI$ = Current market value of all outstanding equity shares

mPj = Current market value of new shares.

k = Discount rate.

I = total investment.

X = total net profit of the firm.

CRITICISM

1. The assumption of perfect capital market is never found in practice.
2. No floatation post and no time lag assumptions are also unrealistic.
3. Assumption of no tax is impractical. There is generally a difference in tax rate applicable to dividend incomes and capital gains in the hands of the shareholders.
4. MM have assumed that the investment policy of the firm is independent of the financing policy. But, some of the firms may undertake only limited investment projects which can be financed by retained earnings only.
5. The MM model may not hold good if the firm is not able to issue additional equity share capital at the then prevailing current market price when dividends are paid MM concludes that the dividend policy of the firm cannot change the present value of the total stream of dividends.

Legal Considerations

1. Legal Aspects : The important provisions of company law pertaining to dividends are mentioned below:

(*i*) Companies can pay only cash dividends with the exception of bonus shares.

(*ii*) Dividend should be declared or paid by the company out of profits after providing for depreciation.

(*iii*) Specified percentage of profits should be transferred to reserves before dividend declaration.

(iv) Dividends cannot be declared for the past years for which the accounts have been closed.

2. Procedural Aspects : The important events and dates in the dividend payment procedure are :

(i) ***Board Resolution*** : The board of directors should in a formal meeting resolve to pay the dividend.

(ii) ***Shareholders Approval*** : The resolution of the board of directors to pay the dividend has to be approved by the shareholders in the annual general meeting.

(iii) ***Record Data*** : The dividends is payable to shareholders whose names appear . in the Register of Members as on the record date.

(iv) ***Dividend Payment*** : Once a dividend declaration has been made, dividend warrants must be posted within 30 days. Within a period of 7 days, after the expiry of 30 days, unpaid dividends must be transferred to a special account opened with scheduled bank.

Dividend Perception in India

The top five determinants of dividend policy, according to the Indian managers are :

1. Current earnings
2. Pattern of past dividends
3. Expected future earning
4. Increasing equity base, and
5. Liquidity.

Managers in India strongly believe that a company should strive to maintain an uninterrupted record of dividend payment and follow a stable pattern of dividend payment. The companies should have target payout ratios, and should not change their dividend policies if they cannot maintain it and is believed that current dividend depends, in part, on current earnings and in part on dividend paid in previous years.

In the view of managers, payment of dividends helps to communicate the future prospects of the company, and dividends should be paid even though companies may have fund requirements for investing in profitable investment opportunities.

ILLUSTRATIONS

Example 1. *The following information i.e., available in respect of the. rate of return on investments (r) the capitalization rate (Ke). and earnings per share. (E) of Ltd.*

r = –(i), 12 %, (ii) 11%, (iii) 8%

K_e–11% and EPS - Rs. 20.00

Calculate market price of the share under following payout ratios. Different payout ratio - 0%, 70%, 25%, 50%, 75% 100%

Solution : According to Walter Model

$$P = \frac{D + (E - D)r / k}{k}$$

D = Dividend per share

= Earnings x Dividend payout ratio $EPS \times (l - b)$

WN–I

Calcualtion of divident per share *Given earnings EPS (or) E = 20.00*

Dividend Payout Ratio (1 - b)	0%	10%	25%	50%	75%	100%
Dividend per share DPS (or) D = E(1-b)	0	2.00	5.00	10.00	15.00	20.00
Retained earnings (E - D) (Or) E x b	20.00	18.00	15.00	10.00	5.00	0

Wn–II

Given *K*	11%	11%	11%
When *r*	12%	11%	8%
rK	1.09	1	0.73

Calculation of market value of Share

When (1-b) / r	0%	10%	25%	50%	75%	100%
12%	$\frac{0+1.09(20)}{0.11}$ = 198	$\frac{2+1.09(18)}{0.11}$ = 197	$\frac{5+1.09(15)}{0.11}$ = 194	$\frac{10+1.09(10)}{0.11}$ = 190	$\frac{15+1.09(5)}{0.11}$ = 186	$\frac{20+1.09(0)}{0.11}$ = 182
11%	$\frac{0+1(20)}{0.11}$ = 182	$\frac{2+1(18)}{0.11}$ = 182	$\frac{5+1(15)}{0.11}$ = 182	$\frac{10+1(10)}{0.11}$ = 182	$\frac{15+1(5)}{0.11}$ = 182	$\frac{20}{0.11}$ = 182
8%	$\frac{0+0.73(20)}{0.11}$ = 133	$\frac{2+0.73(18)}{0.11}$ = 138	$\frac{5+0.73(15)}{0.11}$ = 145	$\frac{10+0.73(10)}{0.11}$ = 157	$\frac{15+0.73(5)}{0.11}$ = 170	$\frac{20}{0.11}$ = 182

2. The implication of dividend policy according to Gordon model respectively for the growth and normal and declining on market price considering the following date :

Growth	Normal	Declining
r - 75%	*r* - 10%	*r* - 8%
K - 70%	*K* - 10%	*K* - 10%
Eps - Rs. 20	*Eps* - Rs. 20	*Eps* - Rs. 20

Calculate market price at different pay out Ratio's 0%, 25%, 50%, 75%, 100% and Commant

According to Gordon Mode

Po = E(1–b) / k–br

(1-b)	0	25	50	75100
b	100	75	50	250
E(l-b)	0	5	10	1520

Solution :

When (1-b) =>b	0 100	25 75	50 50	75 25	100% 0
R=15*(r > k)	0 Rs. 0	5/ 0.10-0.1125 Rs. –400	10' /0.10-0.075 Rs. 400	15 /0.10-0.0375 Rs. 240	20 /0.10-0 Rs. 200
R = 10* (r = k)	0 Rs. 0	5 /0.10-0.075 200	10/0.10-0.05 200	15/0.10-0.025 200	20/0.10-0 200
R = 8% (r < k)	0 Rs. 0	5/0,10-0.06 125	10/0.10-0.04 167	15/0.10-0.02 187.5	20/0.10-0 200

Example 3. *X Engineering company ltd., currently has 1,00,000 shares outstanding selling at Rs. 100 each. The firm is thinking of declaring a dividend Rs, 5 per share at the end the year. The capitalization rate for risk class to which the firm belongs is 10%. What will be the price of the share at the end of the year.*

If a dividend is paid and not paid considering the firms Earnings - Rs. 10,00,000 required new investment Rs. 20,00,000. Solution : Given

n = Existing shares = 1,00,000

P_0 = Issue price per share Rs. 100

D ~ Dividend per share Rs. 5

X = Earnings = Rs. 10,00,000

I = Investment = Rs. 20,00,000

When dividend are not declared i.e., D = Rs. 0

Step No. 1 : Calculation of market price per share (Pi)

$P_1 = P_0(1+K)-D$

P_1 = 100 (1+0.1) = 0 .

P_1 = 100 (1.1)

P_1 = Rs. 110

Step No. 2 : Calculating new no. of shares (m) :

$m = 1-x + n.D/P1$

m = 20,00,000 -10,00,000 + 1,00,000 (0)/110

m = 10,00,000 + 0/110 = 10,00,000/110

m = 9090 shares

Step No. 3 : *Calculation of value of the firm*

$V = n.D + (n + m)Pi - mP1 / 1+k$

10,00,000(0) + (1,00,000 + 9,090)110 - 9,090 (110)/ 1.1

= 1,19,99,900–9,99,900 /1.1

1,10,00,000/1.1

100 00 0000

Calculation Value of Share when Dividend are Paid i.e., D = Rs. 5

Step No. 1 : Calculation Market price per share (Pi)

$PI = P_0(1+K)\text{-}D$

PI = 100 (1 + 0.1) – Rs. 5

PI = 100 (1.1) –5

PI = 110–5 = Rs. 105

Step No. 2 : Calculation new no. of shares (m)

$m = I - X + n.D / P_1$

20,00,000–10,00,000 + 1,00,000(5)/105

m = 14285 shares

Step No. 3 : Calculating value of the firm

$V = n.D + (n + m)Pi - mP1 / 1+k$

= *Rs.* 1,00,000 (5) + (1,00,000 +14,285) 105 –14,285 (105) / 1.10

Rs. 5,00,000 + 1,19,99.925 –14,99,925/ 1.10

Rs 1,00,00,000

CHAPTER 4

Current Assets Management

A. WORKING CAPITAL MANAGEMENT

Working Capital Management

Introduction, Importance, Concepts

Working capital management or short-term financial management is concerned with decision relating to current assets and current-liabilities. Management of working capital refers to the management of current assets as well as current liabilities.

IMPORTANCE OF WORKING CAPITAL

'Working capital management is a significant facet of financial management. Its importance stems from two reasons :

- Investment in current assets represents a substantial portion of total investment
- Investment in current assets and the level of current liabilities have to be decided quickly to changes in sales.

Arranging short-term financing, negotiating favourable credit terms, controlling the movement of cash, administering accounts receivable, and investing short-term surplus funds consume a great deal of time of financial managers.

CONCEPTS OF WORKING CAPITAL

There are two concepts of working capital:

1. Gross Working Capital
2. Net Working Capital

1. Gross Working Capital: Gross working capital is the total of all current assets.

2. Net Working Capital: Net Working Capital refers to the difference between current assets and current liabilities. Current liabilities are those claims of outsiders which are expected to mature for payment within an accounting year and include creditors (accounts payable), bills payable, and outstanding expenses. Net working capital can be positive or negative. A positive net working capital will arise when current assets exceed current liabilities. A negative net working capital occurs when current liabilities are in excess of current assets.

Net working capital is expressed as follows :

Net working capital = current assets - current liabilities.

Determinants of Working Capital

The working capital needs of a firm are influenced by numerous factors. The important ones are :

- Nature of business
- Seasonally of operations
- Production policy
- Market conditions
- Conditions of supply

1. Nature of Business: The working capital requirement of a firm is closely related to the nature of its business. A service firm, like an electricity undertaking or a transport corporation, which has a short operating cycle and which sells predominantly on cash basis, has a modest working capital requirement. On the other hand, a manufacturing concern like a machine tools unit, which has a long operating cycle and which sells largely on credit, has a very substantial working capital requirement.

2. Seasonality of Operations: Firms which have marked seasonality in their operational usually have highly fluctuating working capital requirements.

3. Production Policy: A firm marked by pronounced seasonal fluctuations in its sales may pursue a production policy which may reduce the sharp variations in working capital requirements.

4. Market Conditions: The degree of competition prevailing in the market place has an important bearing on working capital needs. When competition is keen, a larger inventory of finished goods is required. Generous credit terms may have to be offered to attract customers in a highly competitive market. Thus, working capital requirements tend to be high because of greater investment in finished goods inventor and accounts receivable.

If the market is strong and competition weak, *a* firm can manage with a smaller inventory of finished goods.

5. Conditions of Supply: The inventory of raw materials, spares, and stores depends on the conditions of supply. If the supply is prompt and adequate, the firm can manage with small inventory. If the supply is unpredictable and is in shortage. The firm may required high levels of stock and hence higher working capital.

Level of Current Assets and their Financing: Current assets and current liabilities are those which are convertible/payable into cash within a short span of time usually 1 year.

The two concepts of working capital—gross and net—have equal significance from the management viewpoint. The gross working capital concept focuses attention on two aspects of current.

1. Level of current assets

2. Financing of current assets.

1. Level of Current Assets

(a) Current Assets Policies: The level of current assets can be measured by relating current asset? to fixed assets. Assuming a constant level of fixed assets, a higher . CA/FA ratio indicates a conservative current assets policy and a lower CA/FA ratio means an aggressive assets policy assuming other factors to be constant. A conservative policy (i.e., higher CA/FA ratio) implies greater liquidity and lower risk; while an aggressive policy (i.e., lower CA/FA ratio) indicates higher risk and poor liquidity. Different current assets policies are shown in the diagram below :

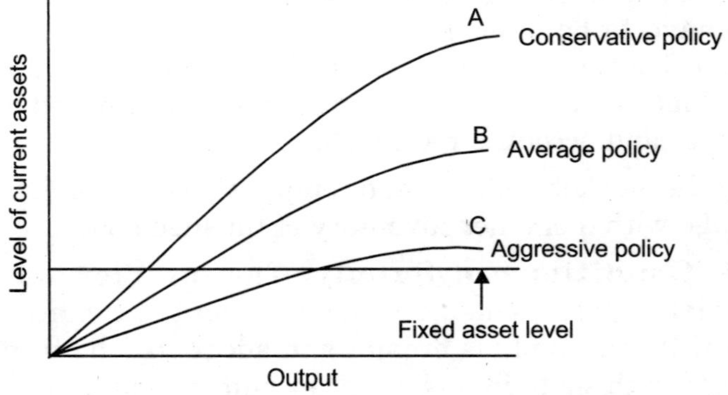

(b) Optimization of Investment in Current Assets Policies: The consideration of the level of investment in current assets should avoid two points—excessive and inadequate investment in current assets. Investment in current assets should be just adequate, not more not less, to the needs of the business firm.

(*i*) Excessive Investment in current assets should be avoided because it impairs the firm's profitability, as investment is idle.

(*ii*) Inadequate investment of working capital threatens so solvency of the firm because of its inability to meet its current obligations.

The working capital needs of the firm may be fluctuating with the changing business activity. The management should be prompt to initiate an action in case of excessive and shortage of funds in current assets.

(*c*) Net working capital is a qualitative concept. It indicates the liquidity position of the firm and suggests the extent to which capital needs may be financed by permanent sources of funds. Current assets should be sufficiently in excess of current liabilities to constitute a margin or buffer for maturing obligations within the ordinary operating cycle of a business. In order to protect their interests, short-term creditors always like a company to maintain current assets twice the level of current liabilities.

(a) A weak liquidity position poses a threat to the solvency of the company and makes it unsafe and unsound. A negative working capital means a negative liquidity, and may prove to be harmful for the company's reputation.

(b) Excessive liquidity is also unfavourable as funds can be diverted to finance other obligations and is usually considered as mismanagement of current assets.

Therefore, prompt and timely action should be taken by management to improve and correct the imbalances in the liquidity position of the firm.

Financing of Current Assets

When a need for working capital funds arises due to increased level of business activity, financing arrangement should be made immediately. Similarly when some surplus funds arise, they should not be allowed to remain idle, but should be invested in short -term securities. There the finance manager should have the knowledge of sources of working capital funds as well as investment avenues where idle funds may be temporarily invested.

(a) Types of Financing: A firm can adopt different financing policies vis-a-vis' current assets. Three types of financing may be distinguished :

- Long-term Financing: The sources of long-term financing include ordinary share capital, preference share capital, debentures, long-term borrowings from financial institutions and reserves and surplus (retained earnings).
- Short-term Financing: The short-term financing is obtained for a period less than one year. It is arranged in advance from banks and other suppliers of short-term finance in the money market Short-term finances include working capital funds from banks, public deposits, commercial paper, factoring of receivable etc.
- Spontaneous Financing: Spontaneous financing refers to the automatic sources of short-term funds arising in the normal course of a business.

SHORT-TERM *VS* LONG-TERM FINANCING

Short term financing may be preferred over long term financing for two reasons:

(*i*) The cost advantages; and

(*ii*) Flexibility. But short-term finances is more risky than long-term financing.

Net working capital concept covers the question of judicious mix of long-term and short-term funds for financing current assets. For every firm, there is a minimum amount of net working capital which is permanent. Therefore, a portion of the working capital should be financed with the permanent sources of funds such as equity share capital, debentures, long-term debt, preference share capital or retained earnings. The portion that is required on a constant basis towards of working capital is called as permanent working capital and the amount over and above permanent working capital is called as temporary or fluctuating working capital. Permanent working capital should always be financed from long-term source and temporary working capital from short-term sources of finance.

(b) Approaches to Financing: Depending on the mix of short and long-term financing the company can follow three approaches.

1. *Matching Approach*: The firm's fixed assets and permanent current assets are financed with long - term funds and as the level of these assets increases, the long-term financing level also increases. The temporary or variable current assets are financed with short-term. funds and as their level increases, the level of 'short-term financing also increases. Under matching plan, no short-term financing will be used if the firm has a fixed current assets need only.

The matching approach is shown below :

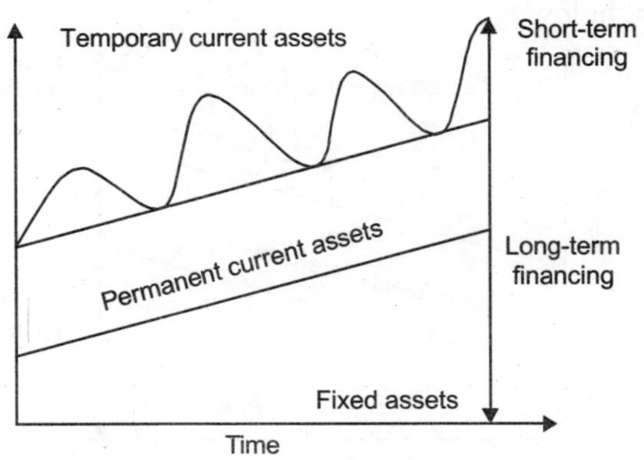

2. *Conservating Approach* : Under a conservation plan, the firm finances its permanent assets and also a part of temporary current assets with long-term financing. In the periods when the firm has no need for temporary current assets, the idle long-term funds can be invested in the tradable securities to conserve liquidity. The conservation plan relies heavily on long-term financing and, therefore, the firm has less risk of facing the problem of shortage of funds. The conservative financing policy is shown in below:

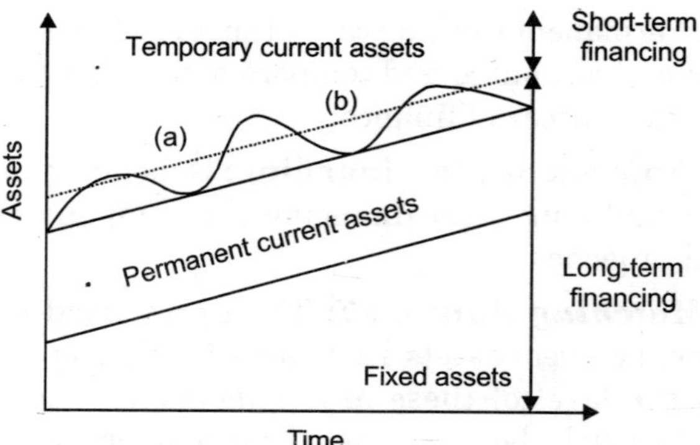

(c) Aggressive Approach : Under an aggressive policy, the firm finances a part of its permanent current assets with short-term financing. Some extremely aggressive firms may even finance a part of their fixed assets with short-term financing. The relatively more use of short-term financing makes the firm more risky. The aggressive financing policy is shown below :

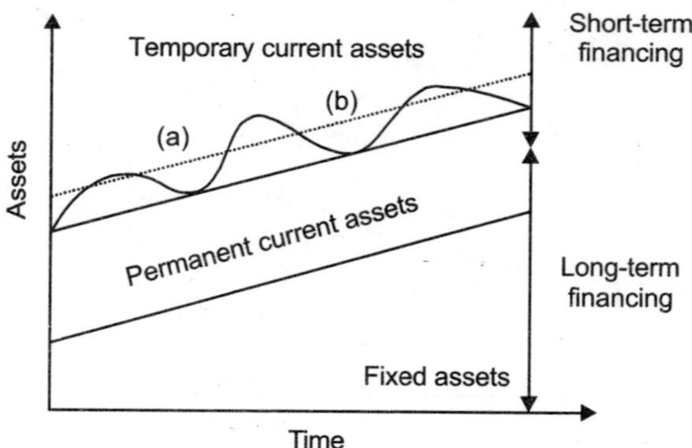

LIQUIDITY *VS* PROFITABILITY : RISK-RETURN TRADE OFF

To estimate working capital needs accurately, the firm must decide about levels of current assets to be carried. Firms may follow a conservative or an aggressive policy. These policies involve risk-return trade-offs. A conservative policy means lower return and risk, while an aggressive policy produces higher return and risk.

The two important aims of the working capital management are : profitability and solvency. Solvency, refers to the firm's continuous ability to meet maturing obligations. Thus, a liquid firm has less risk of insolvency; however, there is cost associated with maintaining a sound liquidity position. A considerable amount of' the firm's funds will be tied up in current assets, and to the extent this investment is idle, the firm's profitability will suffer.

To have higher profitability, the firms may have low level of current assets thus the profitability will improve but solvency is at threat.

Effects of Excessive and Inadequate Working Capital Levels

1. Dangers of Excessive Working Capital

- It results in unnecessary accumulation of inventories. Thus, chances of inventory mishandling, waste, theft and losses increase.
- It is an indication of defective credit policy and slack collection period. Consequently, higher incidence of bad debt results, which adversely affects profits.
- Excessive working capital makes management complacent which degenerates into managerial inefficiency.
- Tendencies of accumulating inventories tend to make speculative profits grow. This may tend to make dividend policy liberal and difficult to cope with in future when the firm is unable to make speculative profits.

2. Dangers of Inadequate Working Capital

- It stagnates growth. It becomes difficult for the firm to undertake profitable projects for non-availability of working capital funds.
- It becomes difficult to implement operating plans and achieve the firm's profit target.

- Operating inefficiencies creep in when it becomes difficult even to meet day-to-day commitments.
- Fixed assets are not efficiently utilized for the lack of working capital funds. Thus, the firm's profitability would deteriorate.
- Paucity of working capital funds render the firm unable to avail-attractive credit opportunities etc.
- The firm loses its reputation when it is not in a position to honour its short-term obligations. As a result, the firm faces tight credit terms.

The management should, therefore, maintain the right amount of working capital on a continuous basis. To ensure proper functioning of business operations. Sound financial and statistical techniques, supported by judgement, should be used to predict the quantum of working capital needed at different time periods.

Operating Cycle

Working capital is the amount required to run the day-to-day business activities. Current assets are needed because sales do not convert into cash instantaneously. There is always an operating cycle involved in the conversion of sales into cash. Investment in current assets such as inventories and debtors (accounts receivable) is realized during the firm's operating cycle which is usually less than a year.

Operating cycle is the time duration required to convert sales, after the conversion of resources into inventories, into cash. The operating cycle of a manufacturing company involves three phases :

- Acquisition of resources such as raw material, labour, power and fuel etc.
- Manufacture of the product which includes conversion of raw material into work-in-progress into finished goods.

- Sale of the product either for cash or on credit. Credit sales create account receivable for collection.

These phases affect cash flows, and cash outflows usually occur before cash inflows.

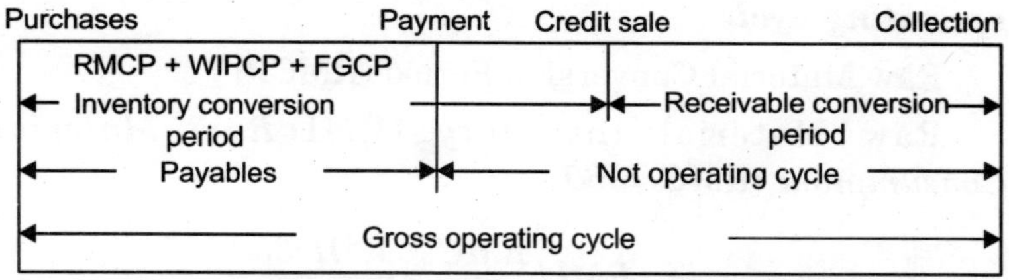

Figure : Operating Cycle of a Manufacturing Firm

The length of the operating cycle of a manufacturing firm is the sum of (*i*) *Inventory conversion period* (ICP) and (ii) Debtors conversion period (DCP)

1. Inventory Conversion Period: The inventory conversion period is the total time needed for producing and selling the product it includes :

(a) *Raw material conversion period* (RMCP).

(b) Work in-process *conversion period* (WIPCP), and

(c) *Finished goods conversion period* (FGCP).

2. Debtors Conversion Period: The debtors conversion period is the time required to collect the outstanding amount from the customers. The total of inventory conversion period and debtors conversion period is referred to as gross *operating cycle* (GOC).

COMPUTATION OF OPERATING CYCLE

The firm's gross operating cycle (GOC) can be determined as inventory conversion period (ICP) plus debtors conversion period (DCP).

Net operating cycle (NOC) is the difference between gross operating cycle and payables deferral period.

Net operating cycle = Gross operating cycle - payables deferral period

$$NOC = GOC - POP$$

$$GOC = ICP + DCP$$

The following formulae can be used for calculating operating cycle

Raw Material Conversion Period (RMCP)

Raw Material Inventory (RMI)/*Raw Material Consumption (RMC) / 360*

$$= RMI / \frac{RMC}{360} = \frac{RMI*360}{RMC}$$

Work-in Process Conversion period (WIPCP)

Work-in Process Inventory (WIPI)/[Cost *of Production (COP) / 360]*

$$= FGI \div COP / 360 = WIPI * 360 / COP$$

Finished Goods Conversion Period (FGCP)

Finished Goodsl Inventory (FGI) ÷ Cost of Goods Sold (CGS)/360

$$= FGI \div CGS / 360 = FGI \times 360 / CGS$$

Debtors Conversion Period (DCP)

$= DEBTORS\ (D) \div Credit\ sales\ at\ cost\ (CRSALES) / 360$

$= D \div CRSALES / 360 = D \times 360 / CRSALES$

Payables, Deferral Period (PDP)

$= Creditors\ (CRS) \div Credit\ Purchase\ (CRPUR) / 360$

$= CRS \div CRPUR / 360 = CRS \times 360 / CRPUR$

Forms of Credit for Working Capital

Credit facility provided by commercial banks to meet the working capital requirement has been an important source of short-term funds to business firms. Bank credit is the main institutional source of short-term financing requirement.

A. Bank Credit : In India, banks may give financial assistance in different shapes and forms. The usual form of bank credit are as follows :

1. **Overdraft:** It is the simplest of different forms of bank credit. In this case, the borrowing firm which already has a current account with the bank is allowed to withdraw more (upto a specified limit) over and above the balance in the current account. The amount so over drawn (i.e., borrowed) may be repaid by depositing back in the current account as and when the firm wants.
2. **Cash Credit:** The credit facility under the cash credit is similar to the overdraft. Under the cash credit, a loan limit is sanctioned by the bank and the borrowing fund can withdraw any amount at any time, within that limit. The interest is charged at the specified rate on the amount withdrawn and for the relevant period. The financing is called cash credit if it is given against the hypothecation of goods or security of the book debts.
3. **Bills Purchased and Bills Discounting:** Commercial banks also provide short-term credit by discounting the bill of exchange emerging out of commercial transactions of sale and purchase. The bill can be discounted by a bank which will pay the amount after charging some discount. The difference between the amount so received and the amount paid by the bank in respect of the bill is the income of the bank.
4. **Letter of Credit:** A letter of credit is a guarantee provided by the buyer's banker to the seller that in case default or failure of the buyer, the bank shall make the payment to the seller. The letter of credit becomes a security of the bill

B. Working Capital Term Loan: Generally, the banks while granting working capital facility to a customer stipulates that a margin of 25% would be required to be provided by the customer and hence the bank borrowing remains only limited to 75% of the security offered.

ILLUSTRATIONS

Example 1. The following data regarding Anna Enterprises is given below. You are required to compute the working capital for the next year after adding 10% to your computed figure towards contigencies : **(Dec. 2005)**

	Rs.
Stock of finished goods	–12,500
stock of stores and raw materials	–20,000
Average credit for domestic sales in 6 weeks	–7,50,000
Average credit for export sales in 4 weeks	–2,00,000
Average time-lag in payments	
Wages 4 weeks	–4,25,000
Stocks 6 weeks	–1,25,000
Rent 3 months	–25,000
Clerical staff 4 weeks	–1,50,000
Executive salaries 4 weeks	–25,000
Miscellaneous expenses 6 weeks	–1,40,000
Payment in advance:	
Sundry expenses paid quarterly	–22,000
Find the average working capital required	

Solution : Determination of Working Capital

	Particulars	Amount
(A)	Current Assets :	
	(i) Stock of finished goods	12,500
	(ii) Stock of stores and raw materials	20,000
	(iii) Sundry expenses [22,000 x 13/52]	5,500
(B)	Debtors :	
	(i) Average credit for domestic sales [750000 x 6/52]	86,538.4
	(ii) Average credit for export sales [2,00,000 x 4/52]	15,384.6
1.	Total current Assets (A + B)	1,39,923
2.	Current Liabilities :	
	Time lag in payments	

Particulars	Amount
(i) Wage [425000*4/52]	32,692.3
(ii) Stock [125,000 x 6/52]	14,423.0
(iii) Rent (25,000 x 13/52]	6,250
iv) Clerical staff [150,000 x 4/52]	11,538.4
(v) Executive salaries [25.000 x 4/52	1,923.0
(vi) Misc. expenses [1,40,000 x 6/52]	16,153.8
Total current liabilities (B)	82,980.5
Networking capital : (1 — 2)	56,942.5
Add : 10% contingencies	5694.25

CASH MANAGEMENT

Introduction

Cash the most liquid asset, is of vital importance to the daily operations of business firm. It is referred to the life blood of a business enterprise.

There are three possible motives for holding cash :

1. **Transaction Motive:** Firms need cash to meet their transaction needs like sale of assets, purchase of goods, acquisition of capital assets and meeting other obligations.
2. **Precautionary Motive:** There may be some uncertainty about the magnitude and timing of cash inflows and cash outflows. To protect against such uncertainties, a firm may require some cash balance.
3. **Speculative Motive:** Firms would like to tap profit making opportunities arising from fluctuations in commodity prices, security prices, interest rates, and foreign exchange rates.

Objective of Cash-Management

The cash management strategies are build around two goals : (*a*) to provide cash needed to meet the obligations; and (b) to minimize the idle cash held by the firm. The financial manager has to strike an acceptable balance between holding too much cash and too little cash. The risk-return trade-off of any firm can be reduced of two prime objectives for the firm's cash management system, as follows:

(i) *Meeting the Cash Outflows* : The firm should be able to make the payments at different point of time without any liquidity problem. It will help the firm in : (a) avoiding the chance of default in meeting financial obligations, otherwise the goodwill of the firm is adversely affected; (b) availing the opportunities of getting cash discounts; and (c) meeting unexpected cash outflows.

(ii) *Minimizing the Cash Balance:* Investment in idle cash balance must be reduced to a minimum. The funds locked up in cash balance has no earning. Therefore, whatever cash balance is maintained, the firm is foregoing interest Income on that balance. The objective of the cash management therefore, should be to keep a minimum cash balance.

Factors Affecting the Cash Needs

To achieve a trade-off between liquidity and profitability there are various factor which will, determine the amount of cash balance to be kept by the firm. Some of these factors are as follows :

(a) Cash Cycle : The term cash cycle refers to the length of the time between the payment for purchase of raw materials and the receipt of sales revenue. So, the cash cycle refers to the time that elapses from the point when the firm makes an outlay to purchase raw materials to the point when cash is collected from the sale of finished goods produced using the raw material.

(b) Cash Inflows and Cash Outflows : Every firm has to maintain cash balance because its expected inflows and outflows are not always synchronized. The timings of the cash inflows may not always match with the timing of the outflows. Therefore, a cash balance is required to fill up the gap arising out of difference in timings and quantum of inflows and outflows.

(c) Cost of Cash Balance : Opportunity cost is another factor to be considered while determining the minimum cash balance. There is always an opportunity cost of maintaining excessive cash balance or inadequate cash by the way of cost of idle funds and cost for raising funds.

Any other considerations, in addition to the above factors which affect the need for cash balance should also be considered while determining cash balance required by a firm.

Etimation of Cash Requirement

The principal method of short-term cash forecasting is the receipts and payments method. The cash budget shows the timing and magnitude of expected cash receipts and payments over the forecast period. It includes all expected receipts and payments irrespective of how they are classified in accounting.

Significance of Cash Budget: Cash budget is an effective tool of cash management and it may help the management in the following ways :

(*a*) Identification of the period of cash shortage and make necessary arrangements.

(*b*) Identification of cash surplus to plan for investment in advance.

(*c*) Better coordination of cash inflows and outflows.

Advantages

(*i*) It provides a complete picture of expected cash flows.

(*ii*) It is a sound vehicle for exercising control over day-to-day transactions.

Drawbacks

(*i*) Its reliability is impaired by delays in collection or sudden demand for large payments and other similar factors.

(*ii*) It fails to provide a clear picture of important changes in the company's working capital movement, especially those relating to inventories and receivables,

Effective Cash Management: The efficient cash management programme should aim at—

(a) Accelerating cash inflows; and

(b) Controlling cash outflows.,

Controlling Inflows : The financial manager should take steps for speedy recovery from debtors. The time lag in collection of receivables can be considerably reduced by managing the time taken by postal intermediaries and banks. Concentration banking and lock box system help reducing this time lag.

A firm may open collection centres (banks) in different parts of the country to save the postal delays. This is known as concentration banking.

Under the Lock box system, the customers mail their payments to a post office box, near their work place. The firm arranges with a local bank or some other agency to collect the payments in order to speed up cash collections.

Controlling Outflows : An effective control over cash outflows or payments also help a firm in better cash management and reducing cash requirements. A financial manager should try to slow down the payments as much as possible. Payments to creditors need not be delayed if it affects trade credits at a later stage.

Optimal Cash Balance Models OPTIMAL CASH BALANCE

The transaction costs will tend to diminish if the cash balance becomes larger. While the opportunity cost of maintaining cash risk as the cash balance increases. Hence, one should achieve a trade off between these costs in order to optimize cash balance.

OPTIMUM CASH BALANCE MODELS

The problem of determining optimum cash balance for a firm implies a trade-off between risk and return of maintaining cash balance. Several models have been suggested to deal with the problem of optimum cash balance. Two important models are as follows:

Baumols Model: This model is the same as the economic order quantity model of the inventory management. This model attempts to balance the income foregone on cash held by the firm against the transaction cost of converting cash into marketable securities or vice-versa.

This model is based on the proposition that in order to reduce the holding cost, a firm keeps the least amount of cash in hand. As the cash level depletes, the firm can acquire cash by selling some of its marketable securities.

Miller-Orr Model: Miller and Orr (1966) have expanded the Baumol's model which is not applicable if the demand for cash is not steady. Where uncertainty over cashflows is large, the inventory type model cannot be used. If balances fluctuate randomly, then a stochastic model can be used to set Control limits.

The model has specified two control limits for cash balance. An upper limit, H, beyond which cash balance need not be allowed to go and a lower limit, L_t below which the cash level is not allowed to reduce. The difference between the higher and lower limits computed by this model is that which minimizes the sum of transaction cost and holding costs.

ILLUSTRATIONS

Example 1. *On first April 2004, the estimated cash balance for a firm is Rs. 40,000. Further details are:*

Particulars	April	May	June	July	August	September
Sales (Rs.)	41,000	45,000	38,000	40,000	53,000	56,000
Material Purchases (Rs.)	12,000	15,500	12,750	16,000	17,500	19,500
Salaries & Wages (Rs.)	6,000	6,500	5,800	13,000	11,500	12,000
Production Overheads (Rs.)	2,400	2,850	2,200	2,250	3,800	4,200
Office & Selling (Rs.) Overhead	2,600	3,300	3,800	4,300	5,400	5,200

The tax rate for the firm is 30%. In the months of May and July payments for the assets acquired are to be paid and they are Rs. 3,800 and Rs. 11,000. Bank loan of Rs. 20,000 is expected in June, 2004. A dividend of Rs. 17,500 is to be paid in October. Debtors are allowed one month's credit and creditors for material purchases and overheads offer one month's credit.

50 per cent of total sales are for cash and salesman's commission of 3 per cent on sales is paid every month. Use the above data and prepare a cash button for six-month period starting from 1st April, 2004.

Solution:

Cash Budget

S.No.	Particulars	April	May	June	July	August	September
I	Opening Balance	40,000	37,289	36,147	48,340	30,373	28,514
II	Receipts Cash sales (or) credit sales	20,500	22,500	19,000	20,000	25,500	28,000
	Collection	—	20,500	22,500	19,000	20,000	26,500
	Bank load	—	—	20,000	—	—	—
	Total Receipts	20,500	43,000	61,500	39,000	46,000	54,500

Payments

	Material	—	12,000	15,500	12,750	16,000	17,500
	Induction OH	—	2,400	2,850	2,200	2-,250	3,800
	Office selling OH	—	2,600	3,300	3,800	4,300	5,400
	Salaries & wages	6,000	6,500	5,800	13,000	11,500	12,000
	Payment of assets	—	3,800	—	11,000	-	—
	Salesman commission	1,230	1,350	1,140	1,200	1,590	1,680
III	Total payment	7,230	28,650	28,590	43,950	35,640	40,380
IV	Closing balance after taxes	37,289	36,147	48,340	30,373	28,514	29,844

Example 2. *Prepare a cash budget in respect of 6 months from July to December from the information given in the table as under:*

Months	Credit	Material	Wages	Production	Administration	Selling	Distribution	Research
April	1,00,000	40,000	10,000	4,400	3,300	1,600	800	1,000
May	1,20,000	60,000	11,200	4,800	2,900	1,700	800	1,000
June	80,000	40,000	8,000	5,600	3,000	1,500	700	1,200
July	1,00,000	60,000	8,000	4,600	2,900	1,400	900	1,200
August	1,20,000	70,000	10,000	5,600	3,000	1,900	1,100	1,400
Sept.	1 ,40,000	80,000	10,000	5,400	3,000	2,000	1,200	1,400
Oct.	1,60,000	90,000	1 0,000	5,800	3,100	2,250	1,250	1,600
Nov.	1,80,000	1,00,000	11 ,000	6,000	3,100	2,150	1,250	1,500
Dec.	2,00,000	1,10,000	11,600	6,400	2,200	2,300	1,500	1,600

1. Cash balance on July 1st was expected to be Rs. 1,50,000
2. **Expected Capital Expenditure:** Plant and machinery to be installed in August at a cost of Rs. 40,000 will be payable of September 1st. Extension to research and development department amounting to Rs. 10,000 will be completed on August, 1st payable Rs. 2000 per month from completion data. Under a hire-purchase agreement Rs. 4,000 is to be paid each month
3. Cash sales of Rs. 2,000 per month are expected.
4. No commission is payable.
5. A sales commission of 5% on (credit) sales is to be paid within the month following the sales.

Period of credit allowed by suppliers	3 months
Period of credit allowed to customers	2 months
Delay in payment of overheads	1 month
Delay in payment of wages	1 month

Income tax of Rs. 1,00,000 is due to be paid on October 1st. Preference share dividend on 10% on 2,00,000 to be paid on November 1st. 10% calls on ordinary share capital of Rs. 4,00,000 is due on July and 1st September.

Dividend from investments amounting to Rs. 30,000 is expected on Nov. 1st.

Solution: Cash Budget For the Ending 31st December

Particular	July	August	Sept.	October	Nov.	Dec.
Opening Balance	1,50,000	2,44,000	2,36,000	2,63,000	1,89,000	2,33,000
ADD : Cash Receipts						
Cash sales	2,000	2,000	2,000	2,000	2,000	2,000
Cash received from Debtors	1,20,000	80,000	1,00,000	1,20,000	1,40,000	1,60,000
DIVIDEND (rec)	—	—	—	—	30,000	—
(4,00,000 x 10%) Call money on ordinary shares	40,000		40,000			
Total of A	3,12,000	3,26,000	3,78,000	3,85,000	3,61,000	3,95,000
Less : Cash Payment						
Payments to creditors	40,000	60,000	40,000	60,000	70,000	80,000
Wages	8,000	8,000	10,000	10,000	10,000	11,000
Production (month) 5,600	4,600	5,600	5,400	5,800	6,000	—
Administration (month)	3,000	2,900	3,000	3,000	3,100	3,100
Selling (months)	1,500	1,400	1,900	2,000	2,250	2,150
Distribution (month)	700	900	1,100	1,200	1,250	1,250
Research & Development	1,200	1,200	1,400	1,400	1,600	1,500
Research & Development (Ex)	—	2,000	2,000	2,000	2,000	2,000
Plant & Machine	—	—	40,000	—	—	—
Hire-Purchase	4,000	4,000	4,000	4,000	4,000	4,000
Sales commission 5%	4,000	5,000	6,000	7,000	8,000	9,000
Preference dividend	—	—	—	—	20,000	—
Income tax	—	—	—	1,00,000	—	—
Total of B -->	68,000	90,000	1,15,000	1,96,000	1,28,000	1,20,000
Closing Batence (A–B) of cash	2,44,000	2,36,000	2,63,000	1,89,000	2,33,000	2,75,000

INVENTORY MANAGEMENT

Introduction, Objectives and Needs

INTRODUCTION

There are three types of inventories : raw materials, work-in-progress, and finished goods. Raw materials are materials and components that are Input in making the final product. Work-in-process, also called stock-in-process, refers to goods in the intermediate stages of production. Finished goods consists of final products that are ready for sale. While manufacturing firms generally hold all the three types of inventories, distribution firms hold mostly finished goods.

OBJECTIVE OF INVENTORY MANAGEMENT

In the context of inventory management the firm is faced with the problem of meeting two conflicting needs :

- To maintain a large size of inventory for efficient and smooth production and sales operations.
- To maintain a minimum investment in inventories to maximize profitability.

Both excessive and inadequate inventories are not desirable. The objective of inventory management should be to determine and maintain optimum level of Inventory investment. The optimum level of inventory will be between the two danger points of excessive and inadequate inventories. .

NEED TO HOLD INVENTORIES

Maintaining inventories involves tying up of the company's funds and incurrence of storage and handling costs. There are three general motives for holding inventories :

- **Transactions *Motive:*** Emphasis the need to maintain inventories to facilitate smooth production and sales operations.
- ***Precautionary Motive:*** Necessitates holding of inventories to guard against the risk of unpredictable changes in demand and supply forces and other factors.
- ***Speculative Motive:*** Influences the decision to increase of reduce inventory levels to take advantage of price fluctuations.

Excessive and Inadequate Investment

The firm should always avoid a situation of over investment or under-investment in inventories.

Dangers of Excessive Investment :

(*a*) Unnecessary tie-up of the firm's funds and loss of profit;

(*b*) Excessive carrying costs; and

(*c*) Risk of liquidity.

Dangers of Inadequate Level of Inventories :

The consequences of under-investment in inventories are :

(a) Production hold-ups; and

(b) Frequent production interruptions, will amount to a loss to the firm.

Effective Inventory Management System : The aim of inventory management, should be to avoid excessive and inadequate levels of inventories and to maintain sufficient inventory for the smooth production and sales operations. Efforts should be made to place an order at the right time with the right source to acquire the right quantity at the right price and quality. An effective inventory management should

- ensure a continuous supply of raw materials to facilitate uninterrupted production
- maintain sufficient stocks of raw materials in periods of short supply
- Minimize total inventory cost, and
- control investment in inventories and keep it at an optimum level.

Inventory Management Techniques : To manage inventories efficienctly one should know :

- How much of quantity should be ordered ?
- When should it be ordered ?

EOQ MODEL

EOQ is the optimum quantity of inventory which must be ordered or produced based on trade off between ordering and carrying costs i.e., quantity the level which the total cost of inventory is minimum.

Determining an optimum inventory level involves two types of costs :

(*a*) Ordering costs; and

(*b*) Carrying costs.

1. Ordering Costs : The term ordering costs is used in case of raw materials (or supplies) and includes the entire costs of acquiring raw materials. They include costs incurred in the activities like requisitioning, purchase ordering, transporting, receiving, inspecting and storing (store placement). Ordering costs.

Ordering costs increase with the number of orders; thus the more frequently inventory is acquired, the higher the firm's ordering costs. On the other hand, if the firm maintains large inventory levels, there will be few orders placed and ordering costs will be relatively small. Thus, ordering costs decrease with increasing size of inventory.

2. Carrying Costs : Costs incurred for maintaining a given level of inventory are called carrying costs. They include storage, insurance, taxes, deterioration and obsolescence.

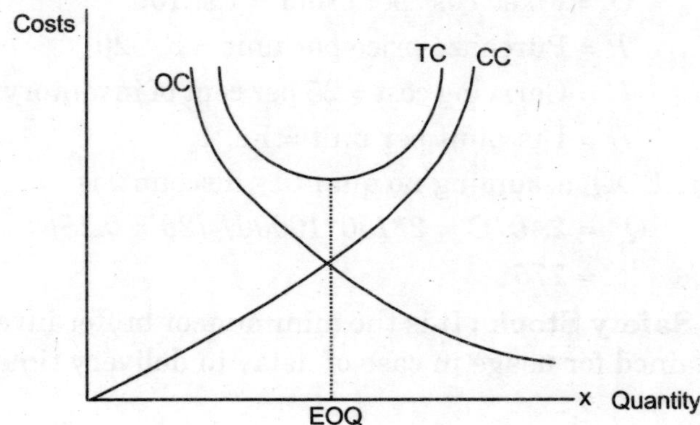

Carrying costs vary with inventory size. This behaviour is contrary to that of ordering costs which decline with increase in inventory size. The economic size of inventory would thus depend on trade'-off between carrying costs and ordering costs.

Assumptions of EOQ Model

1. The demand for given period is known.
2. There is no delay in placing and receiving orders.
3. Two costs are associated with inventory-ordering and carrying costs.
4. The cost per order is constant regardless of the size of order.
5. The cost of carrying is a fixed percentage of average value of inventory.

EOQ Formula :

$$EOQ = \sqrt{\frac{2AO}{C}}$$

Where EOQ = is economic order quantity

A = Annual usuage

O = Cost per order

C = Carrying cost as % of price per unit.

Example : Consider, the following data pertaining to Q limited.

A = annual usage –10,000 units

O = Fixed cost per order = Rs. 150

P = Purchase price per unit = Rs. 20

C = Carrying cost = 25 per cent of inventory value

D = Discount per unit = Re. 1

The EOQ, assuming no quantity discount, is :

$Q^* = 2A0/C = 2*150*10000/\ [20 * 0.25]$

$= 775$

1. Safety Stock : It is the minimum or buffer inventory maintained for usage in case of delay in delivery time.

Maximum possible usage–Normal usage

(Max. usage × Max. lead time)–(Average usage × Average lead time)

2. Reordering Level : The procurement of materials takes time and hence the order level must be such that the inventory at the time of ordering is sufficient to meet the needs of production during the procurement period.

Reorder level = Lead time × Avg. daily usage.

= Max. consumption × max. reorder period

Where lead time is the time for procurement of inventory i.e., time normally taken for receiving the inventory after placing an order.

3. Levels of Inventory

Different levels of inventory can be summarized as follows :

1. Reordering level = Maximum consumption x .Maximum reorder period
2. Minimum stock level = Reorder level–(normal consumption × normal reorder point)
3. Maximum stock level= Reorder level + reordering quantity–(Minimum consumption × Minimum reordering point)
4. Average stock level = $\frac{\text{Minmum level + maximum level}}{2}$

4. ABC Analysis : In most inventories, a small proportion of items accounts for a very substantial usage in terms of the monetary value of annual consumption) and a large proportion of items accounts for a very small usage (in terms of the monetary value of annual consumption). ABC analysis is a system of inventory management which divides inventories into three broad categories, *A, B* and C. Category *A*, representing the most important items, generally consists of 15 to 25 per cent of inventory items and accounts for 60 to

75 per cent of annual usage value. Category *B*, representing items of moderate importance, generally consists of 20 to 30 per cent of inventory items and accounts for 20 to 30 per cent of annual usage value. Category *C*, representing items of least importance, generally consists of 40 to 60 per cent of inventory items and accounts for 10 to 15 per cent of annual usage value. The following figures shows the relationship between cumulative percentage of items and cumulative usage of items.

Figure : Graph of Cumulative Percentage of Items and Cumulative Percentage of Usage

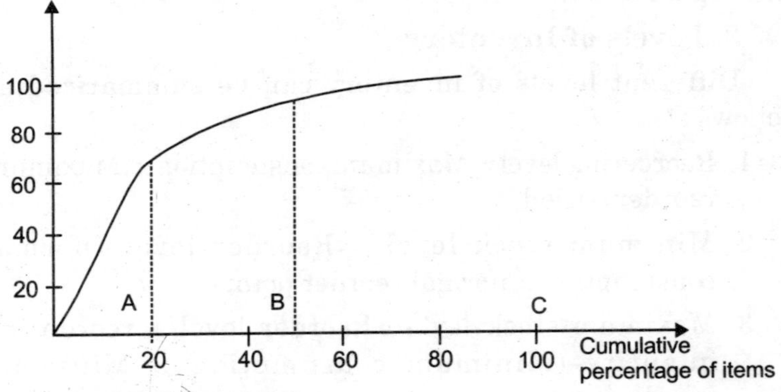

Step in ABC Analysis

1. Classify the Items of inventories, determining the expected use in units and price per unit for each item.
2. Determine the total value of cash item (unit x price).
3. Rank the items according to total value from highest to lowest.
4. Compute percentage of no. of units of each item to total units of all items.
5. Consider cumulative percentages on the basis of relative values to from three categories *A*, *B*, and *C*.

Highest control should be exercised on *A* category moderate control on *B* category and simple control oh *C* category to maximize profits.

5. Just-in-Time Inventory Control : According to just-in-time inventory control system, the firm should maintain a minimal level of inventory and rely on suppliers to provide parts and components *'just-in-time'* to meet its assembly requirements.

Implementation of JIT requires :

(*i*) a strong and dependable relationship with suppliers;

(*ii*) a reliable transportation system; and

Under the 'just-in-time' inventory system, a concerted effort is made to lower the ordering cost, and also the safety stock by forging stronger long-term relationship with the supplier. Keeping the average inventory at lower level.

Example 1. *A manufacturing firm using 12 different types of material has given the following data.*

Items	A	B	C	D	E	F	G	H	I	J	K	L
Units	3,000	32,000	9,000	1600	28,000	11,500	14,600	7,800	11,200	48,000	15,600	13,300
Jnit cost (Rs.)	80	1	42	120	4	10	13.50	8	8.50	3.00	7.50	11.50

(June 2006, Ian. 2005)

Your are *required to present an ABC plan and depict the same graphically.*

Solution :

Items	Units	Cost per unit	Value
A	3,000	80.00	2,40,000
B	32,000	1.00	32,000
C	9,000	42.00	3,78,000
D	1,600	120.00	1,92,000
E	28,000	4.00	1,12,000
F	11,500	10.00	1,15,000
G	14,600	13.50	1,97,100
H	7,800	8.00	62,400
I	11,200	6.50	72,800
J	48,000	3.00	1,44,000
K	1,56,000	7.50	1,17,000
L	13,300	11.50	1,52,950

Items	Units	%	Cumulative %	Value	%	Cumulative %
C	9,000	4.6		3,78,000	20,8	
A	3,000	1.5		2,40,000	13.2	
G	14,600	7.5	45.7 45.7	1,97,000	10.9	71.8 71.8
D	1,600	0.8		1,92,000	10.6	
L	13,300	6.8		1,52,950	8.4	
J	48,000	24.5		1,44,000	7.9	
K	15,600	8.0		1,17,000	6.4	
F	11,500	5.9	28.2 73.9	1,15,000	6.3	18.9 90.7
E	28,000	14.3		1,12,000	6.2	
I	11,200	5.7		72,800	4.0	
H	7,800	4.0	26.1 100	62,400	3.4	9.2 100
B	32,000	16.4		32,000	1,8	
	1,95,600			18,15,250		

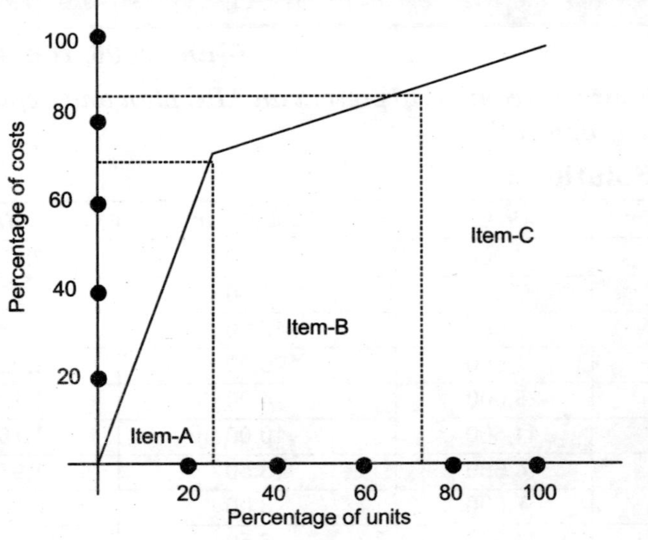

ILLUSTRATIONS

Example 1. *The annual requirement of a material in a firm is 12,600 units. The cost of placing an order is Rs.100* *and the carrying cost is Rs. 0.81 per unit per annum. The following discount schedule is available to the firm :*

(Dec. 2005)

Lot size (units)		Discount in price
1	999	Nil
7000	7999	0.75%
2000	2999	1.10%
3000	4499	1.25%
4500	5999	1.65%
6999	7499	2.00%
7500	9499	2.50%
9500	77499	3.00%
11500 and above		3.50%

Find the EOQ and for that level of EOQ how many orders should be placed in a year.

Solution :

$$EOQ = \sqrt{\frac{2AO}{C}} = \sqrt{2} * 12600 * 100/0.81$$

A = Annual requirement - 12,600 units

O = Ordering cost = 100/-per order

C = earning cost = 0.81

No. of orders = 12600/ 1764 = 7.14 or 7 orders (Appx)

Particular	(No, of orders)								
	1	2	3	4	5	6	7	8	9
Order size	12,600	6,300	4,200	3,150	2,520	2,100	1,800	1,575	1400
Avg. inventory	6,300	3,150	2,100	1,575	1,260	1,050	900	788	700
Carrying cost	5,103	2,552	1,701	1,276	1,021	851	729	638	567
Ordering cost	100	200	300	400	500	600	700	800	900
Total cost	5,203	2,753	2,001	1,676	1,521	1,451	1,429	1,438	1,467
Discount	5,292	3,024	1,890	1,890,	1,663	1663	1,134	1,134	1,134
Net cost after discount	(89)	(272)	111	(214)	(142)	(212)	295	304	(333)

Thus, when the quantity discounts are available, the company should place 7 orders as .the total cost is minimum of Rs. 1,429. It quantity discounts "are available, the firm can place 2 orders as net savings are more.

Example 2. *The finance department of a Corporation provides the following information:*

(i) The carrying costs per unit of inventory are Rs. 10

(ii) The fixed costs per order are Ks. 20.

(iii) The number of units required is 30,000 per year

Determine the economic order quantity (EOQ), the total number of orders to be placed in a year and the time gap between two orders. ***(Jan. 2007)***

Solution :

(2 × 30.000 × 20

$$EOQ = \sqrt{\frac{2AO}{C}} = 346 \text{ units.}$$

No, of orders in a year = 87

Time gap between two orders = about 4 days.

RECEIVABLE MANAGEMENT

Introduction

Trade credit arises when a firm sells its products or services on credit. A firm grants trade credit to protect its sales from the competitors and to attract the potential customers to buy its products. Trade credit creates receivable or book debts which the firm is expected to collect in the near future involving an element of risk.

Receivables constitute substantial portion of current assets. Granting credit and creating debtors amount to the blocking of the firm's funds. The interval between the date of sale and the date of payment has to be financed out of working capital. This necessitates the firm to get funds from banks or other sources. Thus, trade debtors represent investment. Substantial amounts are tied-up in trade debtors and excessive investment leads to opportunity cost. Hence, it needs careful analysis and proper management.

CREDIT POLICY VARIABLES

Credit policy or credit plan lays down the norms and guidelines to determine whether and how much credit is to be extended to a customer.

A firm's investment in accounts receivable depends on :

(a) Decision Variables

(a) The volume of credit sales; and.

(b) The collection period.

The financial manager can affect the volume of credit sales and collection period and consequently, investment in accounts receivables, is through the changes in credit policy. The term credit policy is used to refer to the combination of three decision variables :

(*i*) Credit standards; (*ii*) Credit terms; and (*iii*) Collection efforts.

- **Credit standards** are criteria to decide the types of customers to whom goods could be sold on credit. If a firm has more slow-paying customers, its investment in accounts receivable will increase. The firm will also be exposed to higher risk of default.
- **Credit terms** specify duration of credit and terms of payment by customers. Investment in accounts receivables will be high if customers are allowed extended time period for making payments.
- Collection efforts determine the actual collection period. The lower the collection period, the lower the investment in accounts receivable and vice versa.

(b) Lenient and Stringent Credit Policy

A firm may follow a lenient or a stringent credit policy.

(*i*) A firm following lenient credit policy tends to sell on credit to customers on very liberal terms and standards;

(*ii*) A firm following stringent credit policy sells on credit on a highly selective basis only to those customers who have proven credit worthiness and who are financially strong.

Cost Benefit Analysis

1. Benefits of Granting Credit : The firm uses credit policy for the benefit of :

(*i*) Maintaining or expanding sales.

(*ii*) Maintaining or increasing market share.

2. Costs Associated with Granting Credit : The firm will have to evaluate its credit policy in terms of both return and costs of additional sales. Additional sales should add to the firm's operating profit. There are three types of costs involved :

(*a*) Production and Selling Costs : These costs increase with expansion in sale.

(*b*) Administration Costs : Two types of administration costs are involved when the firm loosens its credit policy:

(*i*) Credit investigation and supervision costs; and (ii) Collection cost.

The firm is required to analyze and supervise large number of accounts when it loosens its credit policy. Similarly, the firm will have to intensify its collection efforts to collect outstanding bills from financially less sound customers.

(*c*) Bad-Debt Losses : Bad-debt losses arise when the firm is unable to collect its account receivable.

Thus the evaluation of a change in a firm's credit policy involves analysis of :

- Opportunity cost.
- Collection costs and bad-debt losses

The credit policy is at optimum level when the incremental sales is more than incremental costs.

(*i*) A tight credit policy means rejection of certain types of accounts whose credit worthiness is doubtful. This results into loss of sales and consequently, loss of contributior.. This is an opportunity loss of the firm.

(*ii*) Losse credit policy implies accepting all or some of those accounts which the firm had earlier rejected.

Thus, a lenient credit policy will incur high blockage of funds leading to higher interest, bad debts is collection costs with high sales. A stringent credit policy will incur low blockage of funds leading to lower interest, bad debts and collections costs with decline in sales.

Determinants of Credit Policy, (or) Receivables

In establishing an optimum credit policy, one must consider the important decision variables which influence the level of receivables. The major controllable decision variables include the following :

1. Credit standards and analysis
2. Credit terms
3. Collection policy and procedures.

The impact of changes in major decision variables of credit policy are explained below:

1. Credit Standards and Analysis : Credit standards are the criteria which a firm follows in selecting customers for the purpose of credit extension. The firm may have tight credit standards; that is, it may sell mostly on cash basis, and may extend credit only to the most reliable and financially strong customers. Such standards will result in no bad-debt losses, and less cost of credit administration. But the firm may not be able to expand sales. The profit sacrificed on lost sales may be more than the costs saved by the firm. On the contrary, if credit standards are loose, the firm may have larger sales. But the firm will have to carry larger receivable. The costs of administering credit and bad-debt losses will also increase. Thus the choice of optimum credit standards involves a trade-off between incremental return and incremental costs.

(a) Credit Analysis : Credit standards influence the quality of the firm's customers. There are two aspects of the quality of customers :

(*i*) The time taken by customers to repay credit obligation, and (*ii*) The default rate.

(*i*) The average collection period (ACP) determines the speed of payment by customers. It measures the number of days for which credit sales remain outstanding. The longer the average collection, period, the higher the firm's investment in accounts receivable.

(*ii*) Default rate can be measured in terms of bad-debt losses ratio-the proportion of uncollected receivable. Bad-debt losses ratio indicates default risk. Default risk is the likelihood that a customer will fail to repay the credit obligation.

2. Credit Terms : The stipulations under which the firm sells on credit to customers are called credit terms. These stipulations include :

(a) The credit period; and

(b) The cash discount.

(a) Credit Period *:* The length of time for which credit is extended to customers is called the credit period. It is generally stated in terms of a net date. For example, if the firm's credit terms are 'net 35', it is expected that customers will repay credit obligation not later than 35 days. A firm's credit period may be governed by the industry norms.

(b) Cash Discount: A cash discount is a reduction on payment offered to customers to induce them to repay credit obligations within a specified period of time, which will be less than the normal credit period. It is usually expressed as a percentage of sales. Cash discount terms indicate the rate of discount and the period for which it is available. If the customer does not avail the offer, he must make payment within the normal credit period.

For example, credit terms may be expressed as '2.5/15, net 40'. This means that a 2.5 per cent discount will be granted if the customer pays within 15 days; and no discount after 15 days and customer should repay credit obligation not later than 40 days.

A firm uses cash discount as a tool to increase sales and accelerate collections from customers. Thus the level of receivable and associated costs may be reduced. The discounts availed by customers is cost to the company.

3. Collection Policy and Procedures : The collection efforts should, aim at accelerating collections from slow-payers and reducing bad-debts losses. A collection policy should ensure prompt and regular collection.

The collection policy should lay down clear - cut collection procedures.

Monitoring Receivable

A firm needs to continuously monitor and control its receivable to ensure the success of collection efforts. Two traditional methods of evaluating the management of receivable are:

1. Average collection period (ACP)
2. Aging schedule.

1. Average Collection Period : Average collection period i.e.,

$$ACP = DEBTORS \times 360 / \; CREDIT\; SALES$$

The average collection period so calculated is compared with the firm's stated credit period to judge the collection efficiency. The average collection period measures the quality of receivable since it indicates the speed of their collectability.

Limitations

(*i*) It provides an average picture of collection experience and is based on *aggregate data.*

(*ii*) It is subject to sales variations.

2. Aging Schedule : The aging schedule removes one of the limitations of the average collection period. It breaks down receivables according to the length of time for which they have been outstanding. It helps to spot out the slow-paying debtors. However, it also suffers from the problem of aggregation.

ILLUSTRATIONS

Example 1. XYZ Limited is selling a product @ Rs. 12 per unit. The total credit sales for the last year were 45,000 units. The variable cost per unit is Rs. 8 and for this level of activity the average cost per unit is Rs. 10. Total fixed costs are Rs. 72,000 and average collection period is 30 days.

The Management is planning to relax the credit standards which would increase the sales by 15 % and average collection period to 45 days. The working capital is expected to increase by Rs. 14,000 with collection expenses being same. The required return on investment for the firm is 14%. Do you advise the management to relax the credit standard ?

Similar moeld in June 2006, Aug. 2005, 2004, Oct. 02

	Current	**Future**
Sales units	45,000	51,750
Sales Rs. (12) (–) Variable cost (8)	5,40,000 3,60,000	6,21,000 , 4,14,000
Contribution (–) Fixed cost	1,80,000 72,000	2,07,000 72,000
Total cost	1,08,000	1;35,000

	Current	Future
Collection period .-. Debtors turn over ratio	20 days 360/30	45 days 360 /45
	12	8

Increase in Profit = Rs. 27,000

$$\text{Average-investment in debtors} = \frac{\text{Cost of goods sold}}{\text{Debtore tumover Ratio}}$$

Average investment in debtors	4,32,000/ 12 = 36,000	4,86,000/ 8 = 60,750
Cost of investmemnt @ 14%	5,040	8,505

	Credit Policy	
	30 days	**45 days**
Profits	1,08,000	1,35,000
(-) Working capital		14,000
(i). Cost of investment	5,040	8,505
	1,02,960	1,12,495

The change in credit policy from 30 days to 45 days will head to an increase in profit of Rs. 9,535 (1,12,495 - 1,02,960). Hence, the credit standard may be relaxed.

Example 2. A company currently has an annual turnover of Rs. 12,00,000 and an average collection period of 30 days. The company wishes to adopt a more liberal credit policy. Which of the following policies would like the company to adopt. ***(Sept 2003)***

Credit policy	Increase in credit period	Increase in sales	% of default
1.	15 days	Rs. 1,00,000	1%
2.	30 days	Rs. 1,50,000	2.5%
3.	45 days	Rs. 3,00,000	3%
4.	60 days	Rs. 3,50,000	8%

The selling price of the product is Rs. 5, average cost per unit at current level is Rs. 4 and the variable cost per unit is Rs. 3. There are no bad debts now and the cost of capital is 15%.

Solution :

Particulars Credit period (in days)	Present 30	1 45	2 60	3 75	4 90
No. of units @ 5.00	2,40,000	2,60,000	2,70,000	3,00,000	3,10,000
Sales (S) (Units x 5.00)	12,00,000	13,00,000	13,50,000	15,00,000	15,50,000
Variable cost (VC) (Units x 3.00)	7,20,000	7,80,000	8,10,000	9,00,000	9,30,000
Contribution (S.VC)	4,80,000	5,20,000	5,40,000	6,00,000	6,20,000
Fixed cost	2,40,000	2,40,000	2,40,000	2,40,000	2,40,000
1. Profit	2,40,000	2,80,000	3,00,000	3,60,000	3,80,000
2. Investment in DRS Cost * ACP 360	80,000	1,30,000	1,80,000	2,50,000	3,10,000
3. Cost of investment in debtors @ 5%	12,000	19,500	27,000	37,500	46,500
4. Bad debts on sales	—	13,000	33,750	45,000	1,24,000
Net profit [1 – (3 + 4)]	22,8000	2,47,500	2,39,250	2,77,500	2,09,500

From the above table, the company earns maximum profit according to proposed 3rd credit policy. Hence the company is suggested to releax its credit policy from 30 to 75 days.

CHAPTER 5 Corporate Restructures

CORPORATE RESTRUCTURING

Introduction

Business combination may take forms of mergers, acquisitions, amalgamation and takeovers are important features of corporate structural changes playing an important role in the external growth of leading companies.

Major Forms of Restructuring

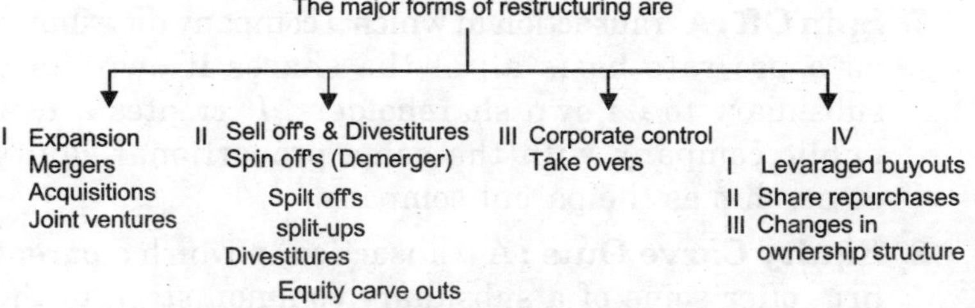

1. **Merger :** It is the combination of two or more companies. One or more companies may merge with an existing company (or) they are merge to form a new company. Amalgamation is used synonymous with merger.
2. **Acquisition :** An acquisition may be defined as an act of acquiring effective control by one company over assets or management of another company without any

combination of companies. Thus, in an acquisition two or more companies may remain independent, separate legal entity, but there may be change in control of companies.'The purchase of a controlling interest in a firm generally through tender offer for the target shares.

3. **Joint Ventures :** Joint venture is a combination of assets contributed by two or more business entities for a specific business purpose and a limited duration. Each of the venture partners continue to exist as a separate firm, and the joint venture represents a new business enterprise.
4. **Divestiture :** Sale of a segment of a company to a third party for cash and/or securities.
5. **Split Off :** The shareholders of parent company will be receiving shares of subsidiary company in return for relinguishing parent company share.
6. **Split Up :** A transaction in which a company spins off all of its subsidiaries to its shareholders and ceases to exist.
7. **Spin Off :** A transaction in which a company distributes on a pro rate basis all of the shares it owns in a subsidiary to its own shareholders. It creates a new public company with the same proportional equity ownership as the parent company.
8. **Equity Carve Outs :** A transaction in which a parent firm offer some of a subsidiary common stock to the general public, to bring in a cash infusion to the parent without loss of control.
9. **Share Repurchase :** A public corporation buys its own shares, by tender offer on the open market or in a negotiated buy back from a large block holder.
10. **Leveraged Buyout :** The purchase of a company by a small group of investors financed largely by debt. Usually entails going private.

Rationale for Business Alliances

Business alliances are motivated by a desire to share risk and' gain access to new markets, reduce costs, receive favourable regulatory treatment, or acquire (or exit) a business.

1. Sharing Risks and Resources : Developing new technologies can be very risky and expensive proposition. Further, such endeavours require pooling technical capabilities of different organizations. Hence, firms in high technology industries form business alliances so that diverse know-how can be pooled, adequate funding can be arranged, and acceptable risk sharing mechanisms can be worked out.

2. Access to New Markets : The cost of accessing a new market may be prohibitive because huge outlays, are required on advertising, promotion, warehousing, and distribution. A company may enter into an alliance to market its products or services through the sales force, distribution outlets, or Internet site of another firm.

3. Cost Reduction : Business alliances can help in reducing costs through sharing or combining of facilities in joint manufacturing operations and mutually beneficial purchaser supplier relationships.

4. Prelude to Acquisition of Exit : A JV or strategic alliance may be a prelude to acquire another company. Alternatively, it may be used as a means for exiting a business.

Forms and Types of Mergers

Merger or Amalgamation may take two Firms

1. **Absorption :** An absorption is a combination of two or more companies into an existing company when the other merging companies will lose their identity.
2. **Consolidation :** A consolidation is a combination of two or more companies into a new company. In this

form of merger, all companies are legally dissolved and a new entity is created. In a consolidation, the acquired company transfers its assets, liabilities and shares to the acquiring company for cash or exchange of shares.

Forms of Merger

1. Horizontal Merger : This is a combination of two or more firms in similar type of production, distribution or area of business.

2. Vertical Merger : This is a combination of two or more firms involved in different stages of production or distribution.

3. Conglomerate Merger : This is a combination of firms engaged in unrelated lines of business activity.

Motives and Benefits of Mergers

A number of reasons are attributed for the occurrence of mergers and acquisitions. Mergers and acquisition are intended to :

- Limit competition
- Utilize under-utilized market power
- Overcome the problem of slow growth and profitability in one's own industry.
- Achieve diversification.
- Gain economies of scale and increase income with proportionately less investment.
- Establish a transnational bridgehead without excessive start-up costs to gain access to a foreign market.
- Utilize under-utilized resources—human and physical and managerial skills.
- Displace existing management.
- Circumvent government regulations
- Reap speculative gains attendant upon new security issue or change in P/E ratio

- Create an image of aggressiveness and strategic opportunism, empire building and to a mass vast economic powers of the company.

The most common motives and advantages of mergers and acquisitions are :

- Maintaining or accelerating a company's growth, particularly when the internal growth is constrained due to paucity of resources;
- Enhancing profitability, through cost reduction resulting from economies of scale, operating efficiency and synergy;
- Diversifying the risk of the'company, particularly when it acquires those business whose income streams are not correlated;
- Reducing tax liability because of the provision of setting-off accumulated losses and unabsorbed depreciation of one company against the profits of another;
- Limiting the severity of competition by increasing the company's market power.

Financial Evaluation

Financial evaluation of a merger is needed to determine the earnings and cash flows, areas of risk, the maximum price payable to the target company and the "best way to finance the merger. The acquiring firm must pay a fair consideration to the target firm for acquiring its business. A merger is said to be at a premium when the offer price is higher than the target firm's pre-merged market value. The acquiring firm may pay the premium if it thinks that it can increase the target firm's after merger by improving its operations and due to synergy.

VALUE CREATED BY MERGER

A merger will make economic sense to the acquiring firm if

its shareholders benefits. Merger will create an economic advantage (EA) when the combined present value of the merged firms is greater than the sum of their individual present values as separate entities. For example, if firm *P* and firm *Q* merge, and they are separately worth *Vp* and *VQ*, respectively, and worth *VPQ* in combination, then the economic advantage will occur if:

$$VPQ > (VP + VQ)$$ •

Significance of EPS and P/E Ratio

Investors attach a lot of importance to the earnings per share (EPS) and the price earnings {P/E} ratio. The product EPS and P/E ratio is the market price per share. • In addition to the market price and the discount value of shares, the mergers and acquisitions decisions are also evaluated in terms of EPS, P/E ratio, book value etc. The negotiations would usually be in terms of exchange of shares which is given below :

Exchange Ratio

The current market values of the acquiring and the acquired firms may be taken as the basis for exchange of shares. As discussed earlier, the Share Exchange Ratio (SER) would be as follows :

Share exchange ratio = Share price of the acquired firm / share price of the acquiring firm

$$Pb / P_a$$

Legal Procedures

The following is the summary of legal procedures for merger of acquisition laid down in the Companies Act, 1956:

Permission for Merger : Two or more companies can amalgamate only when amalgamation is permitted under their memorandum of association. Also, the acquiring company should have the permission in its object clause to carry on the business of the acquired company. In the absence of these provisions in the memorandum of association, it is necessary to seek the permission of the shareholders, board of directors and the Company Law Board before affecting the merger.

Information to the Stock Exchange : The acquiring and the acquired companies should inform the stock exchanges where they are listed about the merger.

Approval of Board of Directors : The boards of the directors of the individual companies should approve the draft proposal for amalgamation and authorize the managements of companies to further pursue the proposal.

Application in the High Court : An application for approving the draft amalgamation proposal duly approved by the board of directors of the individual companies should be made to the High Court. The High Court would convene a meeting of the shareholders and creditors to approve the amalgamation proposal. The notice of meeting should be sent to them at least 21 days in advance.

Shareholder's and Creditor's Meetings : The individual companies should hold separate meetings of their shareholders and creditors for approving the amalgamation scheme. At least, 75 per cent of shareholders and creditors in separate meeting, voting in person or by proxy, must accord their approval to the scheme.

Sanction by the High Court : After the approval of shareholders and creditors, on the petitions of the companies, the High Court will pass order sanctioning the amalgamation scheme after it is satisfied that the scheme is fair and reasonable. If it deems so, it can modify the scheme. The date of the court's hearing will be published in two newspapers, and also, the Regional Director of the Company Law Board will be intimated.

Filing of the Court Order : After the Court order, its certified true copies will be filed with the Registrar of Companies.

Transfer of Assets and Liabilities : The assets and liabilities of the acquired company will be transferred to the acquiring company in accordance with the approved scheme, with effect from the specified data.

Payment by Cash or Securities : As per the proposal, the acquiring company will exchange shares and debentures and/or pay cash for the shares and debentures of the acquired company. These securities will be listed on the stock exchange.

Takeovers

A takeover generally involves the acquisition of a certain block of equity capital of a company which enables the acquirer to exercise control over the affairs of the company. Effective control can be exercised with a smaller holding, usually between 20 and 40 per cent, because the remaining shareholders, scattered and ill-organized, are not likely to challenge the control of the acquirer.

Regulation of Takeovers

Takeovers may be regarded as a legitimate device in the market for corporate control provided they are properly regulated by the following principles :

1. Transparency of the Process : A takeover affects the interests of many parties and constituents such as shareholders, employees, customers, suppliers, contending acquires, creditors, and others. Hence it should be conducted in an open manner. If the process is transparent, takeover will be regarded by various constituents as a legitimate device in the market for corporate control.

2. Interest of Small Shareholders : In a takeover the 'controlling block' which often tends to be between 20 and 40 per cent is usually acquired from a single seller.

3. Realization of Economic Gains : The primary rationale for takeovers should be to improve efficiency of operations and promote better utilization of resources.

4. No Undue Concentration of Market Power : While the regulatory framework must be conductive to the realization of economic gains, it must prevent concentration of market power. The acquirer should not, as a result of the takeover, enjoy undue market power which can be used to the detriment of customers and others.

ANTI- TAKEOVER DEFENCES

A wide range of anti-takeover defences have been employed by target companies to ward off bidders.

ANTI-TAKEOVER DEFENCES IN INDIA

In order to ward off a takeover attempt, companies in India presently invoke one or more of the following defences :

1. Make Preferential Allotment : A company may allot equity shares or convertible securities on a preferential basis to the promoter group so that Its equity stake is enhanced.

2. Effect Creeping Enhancement : As per SEBI guidelines, the prompter group can raise its equity holding by creeping enhancements, subject to limits, without invoking the provision to make an open market offer.

3. Amalgamate Group Companies : Two or more companies promoted by the same group may be amalgamated to form a larger company. Other things being equal, a larger company is less vulnerable to a takeover in comparison to a smaller company.

4. Sell the Crown Jewels : If the raider is tempted by certain valuable assets of the target company, the target company may sell those assets to make itself unattractive.

Example 1. Fertilizers Company is taking over Y Petrochemical Company. The shareholders would receive 0.8 shares of X for each shares held by them. The merger is not expected to yield in economics of scale and operating synergy. The relevant data for the two companies are as follows:

	X	Y
Net sales (Rs. crore)	335	118
Profit after tax (Rs. crore)	58	12
Number of share (crore)	12	3
Earnings per share (Rs)	4.83	4.00
Market value per share (Rs.)	30	20
Price earnings ratio	6.21	5.00

For the combined company (after merger), you are required to calculate (*a*) EPS, (b) P/E ratio, (*c*) market value per share, (*d*) number of shares, and (*e*) total market capitalization. Also calculate the premium paid by X to the shareholders of Y.

Solution : Premium paid to Y shareholders : Value of each share in X :

0.8-x Rs. 30 = Rs. 24

Value of Y share before merger = Rs. 20

Premium = Rs. 4

Premium percentage = 4/20 = 20 per cent

Number of shares paid to Y shareholders :

3 x 0.8 = 2.4 crore

Number of share of the combined company's :

12 + 2.4 = 14.4 crore

Combined profit after tax :

Rs. 58 + Rs. 12 = Rs. 70 Crore.

Combined EPS = 70/14.4 = Rs. 4.86

Combined price - earnings ratio :

6.21 * 58/70 + 5*12/70 = 6.0

Combined firm's market capitalization :

Market value per share = PEratio x EPS = 6.00 x 4,86 = Rs. 29.16

Capitalization : MVPS x No. of shares

= Rs. 29.16 x 14.4 = Rs. 419.9 crore.

Example 2. A Company has decided to acquire B company. The following are the relevant financial data for the two companies :

Calc'ılate

	A	B
Net sales (Rs. lakh)	350	45
Profit after tax (Rs. lakh)	28.13	3.75
Number of share (lakh)	7.50	1.50
Earnings per share (Rs)	3.75	2.5
Dividend per share (Rs.)	1.30	0.60
Totaf market capitalization (Rs. lakh)	420	45

(*a*) Pre-merger market value per share for both companies,

(*b*) Post-merger EPS, market value per share and price - earnings ratio if Kay's shareholders are offered a share of (*i*) Rs. 30 or (*ii*) Rs. 56, or (*iii*) Rs. 20 in a share exchange for merger.

(c) A EPS if B shareholders are offered Rs. 100.15 per cent convertible debenture for each 3 shares held in B, and

(*d*) Post - merger dividend or interest available to B shareholders with exchange referred in (*b*) *and (c) Assume 50 per cent tax rate.*

Solution:

(a) Pre-merger market value per share = Market capitalization / Number of shares

A: 420/7.5 = Rs. 56

B: 45/1.50 = Rs 30

(b) Share exchange ratio :

(*i*) 30/56 = 0.536

(*ii*) 56/56 = 1.00

(*iii*) 20/56 = 0.357

Number of shares of the surviving company :

(*i*) 7.5 + (0.536 × 1.5) = 8.30

(*ii*) 8.5 + (1 × 1.5) = 9.00

(*iii*) 7.5 + (0.357 × 1.5) = 8.04

Combined EPS : Combined PAT/Combined number of shares

(*i*) (28.13 + 3.75)/8.3 = 3.84

(*ii*) (28.13 + 3.75)/ 9 = 3.54

(*iii*) (28.13 + 3.75)/ 8.4 = Rs.3.97

Combined firm's = PE ratio = weighted average of the individual firm's pre-merger PE ratio

$$\left(\frac{420}{28.13}\right)\times\left\{\left(\frac{28.13}{28.13+3.75}\right)\right\}+\left(\frac{45}{3.75}\right)\times\left\{\frac{3.75}{28.13+13.75}\right\}$$

= 14.93 × 0.882 + 12 × 0.118 - 14.58

Market value per share of the surviving firm :

(*i*) (3.84 × 14.58) = Rs. 56 .

(*ii*) (3.54 × 14.58) = Rs. 51.61

(*iii*) (3.97 × 14.58) = Rs. 57.88

(c) *Number of convertible debentures :*

1.50/ 3 = 0-5 lakhs

Interest on debenture

1.50 × Rs. 100 × 15% = Rs. 7.5 Lakh

Combined profit after tax = 28.13 + 3.75 – 7.5 + 0.5 × 7.5

A EPS after merger = 28.13/7.5 = 3.75

Note : Interest will be deducted from the combined profit but is will save tax at 50 per cent tax rate.

(*d*) Dividend to B's shareholder's after merger :

Exchange of Shares :

(*i*) 0.804 × 1.30 = Rs. 1.05 lakh

(*ii*) 1.50 × 1.30 = Rs. 1.95 lakh

(*iii*) 0.536 ×1.30 = Rs. 0.70 lakh

Interest .0.50 × 100 × 0.15 = Rs. 7.50 lakh

Post-merger dividend :

1.50 × 0.6 = Rs. 0.90 lakh

Example 3. M company is being acquired by *N* Company on a share exchange basis. Their selected data areas follows:

	M	N
Profit after tax (Rs. lakh)	56	21
Number of share (lakh)	10	8.5
Earnings per share (Rs)	5.6	2.5
Price - earnings ratio	12.5	7.5

Determine (*a*) pre-merger, market value per share, and (*b*) the maximum exchange rath M company should offer without the dilution of (*i*) EPS (*ii*) Market value per share.

Solution : (*a*) Pre-emerger market – value per share : = *PE RATIO* × EPS

N : 12.5 × 5.6 = Rs. 70

M : 7.5 × 2.5 = Rs. 18.75

(*b*)(*i*) Maximum exchange ratio without dilution of EPS :

Pre-merger PAT of N (Rs. Lakh)	56
Pre-merger PAT of M (Rs. lakh)	21
Combined PAT without Synergy (Rs. lakh)	77
EPS of M	5.6
Max no of shares of N after merger [77/ 5.6]	13.75
Existing number of shares (lakh)	10.00
Maximum number of shares to be exchanged (lakh)	3.75
Maximum share exchange ratio : 3.75/8.4	0.446

(*ii*) Maximum exchange ratio without dilution of market value per share :

Pre - merger market capitalization of N :	
MV x No. of shares = Rs. 70 x 10 laks	700
Pre - merger market capitalization of M :	
MV x No. of shares = Rs. 18.75 x 8.4 laks	157.5
Combined market capitalization (Rs. lakh)	857.5
Current market value per share for N shareholders (Rs.)	70
Maximum number of shares of N (surviving company)	12.25
Current number of shares of Large (lakh)	10.00
maximum number of shares to be exchanged (lakh)	2.05
Maximum shares exchanged ratio : 2.25/8.4	0.268

Introduction

Value maximization is the central theme in financial management and appraising the value of the firm is important task which needs proper understanding of different approaches to value the firm one of the universally accepted modern approach is discounted cash flow approach

Discounted Cash Flow Approach (DCF Approach)

Valuing a firm using the discounted cash flow approach involves forecasting cash flows over an indefinite period of time for an entity that is expected to grow. Thus the value of the firm is separated into two time periods i.e., the value of firm during growth period i.e., explicit forecast period (EEP) and the firm is expected to reach steady state after the EFP. The following steps are involved in valuing a firm under DCF approach :

1. Forecast the cash flow during the growth period

(*a*) Determine the EFP.

(*b*) Estimate free cash flows to the firm,

(*i*) The free cash flow to the firm {FCF) is the sum of

cash flow to all investor of the firms lenders and shareholders.

FCF = Operating cash flows + Non operating cash flows

Where operating cash flow = Net operating profit after taxes - Net investment

This involves forecasts and projections considering all the key drivers that effect the performance of the firm.

(*ii*) ***Drivers of Free Cash Flow :***

Invested Capital : This is the capital invested in the operating assets of the firm comprising of fixed assets and net working capital.

$\frac{\text{NOPLAT}}{\text{Invested Capital}}$ represents the return on invested capital (ROIC)

$\frac{\text{Net investment}}{\text{Invested Capital}}$ This reflects the growth rate

Thus, invested capital, ROIC, and growth rate are the basic drivers of FCF.R01C, in turn, can be broken down as follows :

$$ROc = \frac{NOPLAT}{Invested\ Capital}$$

$$= \underbrace{\frac{NOPLAT}{Turnover}}_{\substack{Post\text{-}tax \\ Operating\ margin}} \times \underbrace{\frac{Tumover}{Capital}}_{\substack{Capital \\ tumover}}$$

2. Calculate cost of capital using weighted average cost of capital.

$$WACC = r_E\left(\frac{S}{V}\right) + r_P\left(\frac{P}{V}\right) + r_D + (1-T)\left(\frac{B}{V}\right)$$

(or)

$$WACC = w_e k_e + w_p k_p + w_e k_d (1 - t)$$

3. Determine cash flow the continuing value at time steady state

$$CV = \frac{CFAT}{k - g}$$

METHODS OF ESTIMATING CONTINUING VALUE

The following methods are available for estimating the continuing value. They may be classified into two broad, categories as follows :

Cash Flow Methods	Non-Cash Flow Methods
• Growing free cash flow perpetuity	• Replacement cost method
• Value driver method	• Price-EBIT ratio method
	• Market-to-book ratio method

Growing Free Cash Flow Perpetuity Method : This method assumes that the free cash flow would grow at a constant rate forever, after the explicit forecast period, T. Hence, the continuing value of such a stream can be established by applying the constant growth valuation model :

$$CV_T = \frac{FCF_{J+1}}{WACC - g}$$

Where CV_j = Continuing value at the end of year T

$FCFj + 1$ = Expected free cash flow for the first year after the explicit forecast period.

WACC= Weighted average cost of capital

g= Expected growth rate of free cash flow for ever.

(*ii*) Value Driver Method : This method uses the growing free cash flow perpetuity formula but expresses it in terms of value drivers as follows :

$$\mathrm{CV_T} = \frac{NOPLT_{T+1}(1 - g/r)}{WACC - g}$$

CVj = Continuing value at the end of year T

NOPLATj+i = Expected net operating profits less adjusted tax for the first year after the explicit forecast period.

WACC = Constant growth rate of NOPLAT after the explicit forecast period

r = Expected rate of return on net new investment.

(iii) Replacement Cost Method : According to this method, the continuing value is equated with the expected replacement cost of the fixed assets of the company.

(iv) Price-to -PBIT Ratio Method : A commonly used method for estimating the continuing value is the price-to-PBIT ratio method. The expected PBIT in the first year after the explicit forecast period is multiplied by a 'suitable' price-to-PBIT ratio.

(v) Market-to-Book Ratio Method : According to this method, the continuing value of the company at the end of the explicit forecast period Is assumed to be some multiple of its book value. The approach is conceptually analogous to the price PBIT ratio.

On the whole, the cash flow methods, are considered superior to the non-cash flow methods.

4. *Determine value of the firm i.e., present value of future cash flows and interpret results*

Value of firm (V) = PV of FCF during EFP + PV of CV + Value of non-operating assets

APPROACHES TO VALUE BASED MANAGEMENT SYSTEMS

To help firms create value for shareholders, value based management (VBM) approaches have been developed. Several methods have been used and the principal methods of VBM are :

1. Marakon Approach : The Marakon approach is based on a market-to-book ratio model. According to this model, shareholder wealth creation is measured as the difference between the market value and the book value of a firm's equity. The book value of equity, *B*, measures approximately the capital contributed by the shareholders, whereas the market value of equity, *M*, reflects how productively the firm .has employed the capital contributed by the shareholders, as assessed by the stock market. Hence, the management creates value for shareholders if *M* exceeds *B*, decimates value if *M* is less than *B*, and maintains value if *M* is equal to *B*.

According to the Marakon model, the market-to-book values ratio is a function of the return on equity, the growth rate of dividends (as well as earnings), and the cost of equity :

$$\frac{M}{B} = \frac{r-g}{k-g}$$

Where M = market value of equity

B = Book value of equity

r = return on equity

g = growth rate in dividends

k = cost of equity

Equation may be derived from the constant growth dividend discount model. To demonstrate this, we will use the following additional symbols :

P_0 = market price per share at the end of year 0 (P_0 - M)

$D1$ = dividend per share at the end of year 1

b = dividend payout ratio {1 – b) = retention ratio

According to the constant growth dividend discount model :

$$Po = D1/[k-g] = B0\ rb/[k-g]$$
$$= Po/Bo = rb/[k-g]$$

we know $g = (1 - \text{b})\ r$

$$br = r - g$$
$$M = r - g$$
$$= \frac{P_0}{B_0} - \frac{M}{B}$$
$$= \frac{r-g}{k-g}$$

A higher growth rate contributes more to value creation and value is created only when $r > k$ implying higher g. Hence according to this approach return on equity cost of equity and growth rate are financial determinants or drivers of value of the firm.

2. Alcar Approach : The Alcar Group Inc., a management education and software company, developed an approach to VBM which is based on discounted cash flows analysis, regarded by many as the father of shareholder value.

Determinants of Shareholder Value : According to Rappaport the following seven factors called *"value drivers"* that affect shareholder value :

1. Rate of sales growth
2. Operating profit margin
3. Income tax rate
4. Investment in working capital
5. Fixed capital investment.
6. Cost of capital
7. Value growth duration

While the first six "value drivers " are financial yardsticks and value growth duration, represents the period over which investments are expected to earn rates of return in exess of the cost of capital. It is an estimate reflecting the belief of management that competitive advantage will exist for a finite period. Thereafter, the competitive edge would be lost causing the rate of return to regress to the cost of capital. Figure represents the conceptual framework of the Alcar approach.

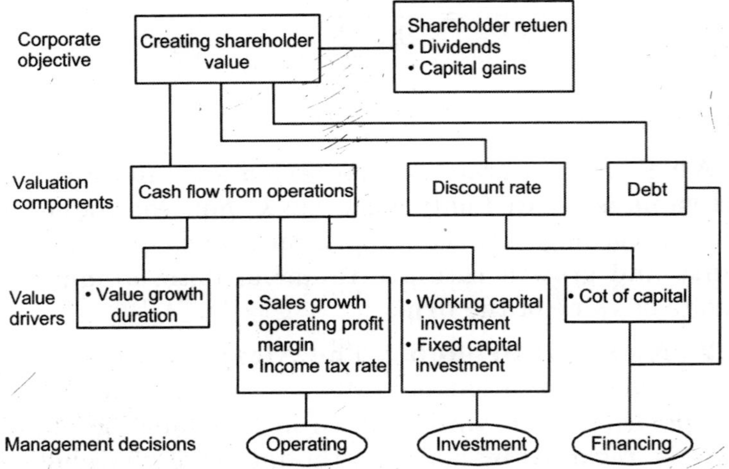

Share holder Value creation Network

The procedure of assessing the shareholders impact of a strategy involves

(*i*) Operating cash flow = Net operating profits after taxes– Net investment

(*ii*) Calculate WACC

(*iii*) Present value of operating cash flows

(*iv*) Estimate present value of residual value =

$$\frac{\text{Perpetuity cash flow}}{\text{Cost capital}}$$

(*v*) Determine the shareholders value

= Present value of operating cash flows and residual value–Market value of debt.

(*vi*) Establish pre strategy value =

$$\frac{\text{Cash flow before investment}}{\text{Cost of capital}}$$

(*vii*) Value created by strategy = total shareholders value– Pre strategy value.

3. McKinsey Approach : McKinsey and Company, a leading international consultancy firm, has developed an approach to VBM which has been very well articulated by Tom Copeland, Tim Koller, and Jack Murrin of McKinsey & Company.

According to this approach, the implementation of VBM is to ensure that senior managers embrace value maximization as the ultimate financial objective. This means that top management should focus on discounted cash flow value (the most direct measure of value creation) and eschew traditional measures like earnings per share, growth in profit, or accounting rate of return as they are often poor proxies for value creation. Considering financial and non financial goals.

An essential ingredient of VBM is a sound understanding of performance variables, referred to as the key value drivers, that influence the value of the business. It is suggested that it is useful to examine value drivers at three levels as mentioned below:

Generic Level : As this level, the return on invested capital is analyzed in terms of operating margin and invested capital.

Business" *Unit Level :* At this level, variables like product-mix, customer-mix, operating leverage, and so on, are relevant.

Grass roots *Level :* At this level, the focus is on operating value drivers like capacity utilization, revenues generated per visit, cost per delivery, and so on, that are directly influenced by the decision of front line managers.

VBM calls for gearing the following managerial processes to value maximization : strategy development, target setting, action plans (budgets), and performance measurement/incentive system and ensuring proper implementation of VBM system.

INTRODUCTION

Managers are the agents of shareholders. There is often a lack of congruence in the objectives of the shareholders (principals) and managers (agents). This leads to agency costs which represent a loss in the value of the firm. It is in interest of principal as well as the agents to find ways and means of minimizing the agency costs.

To mitigate agency costs of variety of devices have evolved. Some are internal and some external. The key internal devices are internal monitoring and incentive compensation contracts. The two important external devices for mitigating agency costs are the market for corporate control and the managerial labour market

Corporate governance is concerned primarily with the agency problem that arises from the separation of finance and management (or, in popular terms, ownership and control). It refers to the mechanisms and arrangements employed by financiers (shareholders and lenders) to induce managers, who tend to acquire considerable residual control rights in practice, to care for their interest.

CORPORATE GOVERNANCE IN INDIA

A great deal of concern has been expressed all over the world about the shortcomings in the systems of corporate governance. The general failure of large companies to restructure and redirect themselves In the absence of external compulsions reflects an inadequacy in the corporate governance mechanisms.

The corporate governance in India may be divided into two parts. The first deals with corporate governance in the private sector, and the second, in the public sector.

Corporate in the Private Sector

The distinctive features of corporate governance in the private sector are as follows:

1. There are three categories of shareholders : promoters, financial institutions and individual investors.
2. For electing the directors, the majority rule voting system is typically followed.
3. Company boards comprise of three types of directors : promoter directors, professional directors, and institutionally nominated directors.
4. Scattered and ill-organized, individual shareholders are not in a position to play a meaningful role in electing directors.
5. Family managed companies, display greater entrepreneurial vigour, act more proactively, and exercise stricter control. The virtually unchallenged control of the family provides enormous scope for self-dealing and facilitates personal enrichment at the expense of the company.
6. Professionally managed companies, react slowly to new opportunities and challenges, put greater emphasis on systems, favour the interest of Incumbent management over that of shareholders, and set relatively easy performance targets.

Corporate Governance in the Public Sector

The salient features of corporate governance in the public sector are as follows:

1. The equity shares are owned wholly or substantially {meaning 51 per cent or more) by the government.
2. The boards of public sector undertakings, appointed for all practical purposes by the controlling administrative ministry, comprise of three categories of directors :
   (*i*) Functional directors
   (*ii*) Government directors
   (*iii*) Outside directors.
3. There is a good deal of political and bureaucratic influence over the management of public sector undertakings. As a result, the autonomy of the management is often eroded.
4. Public sector undertakings are constrained by various regulations and administrative guidelines. This leads to an excessive emphasis on observing rules, regulations, and guidelines. Efficiency and performance are often affected.
5. Performance standards are soft, compensation levels low, incentives for performance poor, and 'real' accountability weak.

Principles of Good Corporate Governance

1. **Strengthen the Role of Institutional :** Investors financial institutions which currently have substantial equity and debt exposure in companies should play a more active role in monitoring companies, chastening wayward managements, and instilling confidence in the ordinary investor.
2. **Separation of Management and Control Functions :** The function of management i.e., proposals for managing resources of the firm, their

evaluation and approval aspects must vest with the chief executive officer and his team and the function of control i.e., execution of approved proposals and rewarding executives by assessing their performance with the board of directors. Such a separation of control and management helps in mitigating the agency problem.

3. **Expand the Role of Non-executive Directors :** Non-executive directors can bring varied expertise, rich experience, and a certain degree of objectivity in monitoring corporate behaviour. Their role needs to be expanded to improve the quality of corporate governance.

4. **Limit the Size of the Board :** As the size of the board increases, it becomes less effective because the advantages of wider participation are outweighed by the problems of coordination. Hence, It is advisable to ordinarily limit the size of boards to seven or so. Any board which has more than ten to twelve directors tends to become unwieldy and inefficient.

5. **Ensure that the Board is Information ally Well-equipped :** The board of directors should receive information about the performance of the company in all important areas. The power of a board to influence the course of corporate affairs lies not in legal or organizational authority, but in access to the information that compels attention and demonstrates the need for change.

6. **Link Managerial Compensation to Performance :** Agency problems arise because of lack of alignment of the interests of shareholders and management. To make these interests more congruent, a significant portion of managerial compensation should be linked to the value created by management.

7. **Introduce Cumulative Voting System :** The principal difference between the majority rule voting

system and cumulative voting system is that under the former, the board can be completely dominated by the principal controlling group, whereas under the latter a significant minority, if it casts its votes intelligently, is assured of some representation on the board improve corporate governance.

8. **Improve Corporate Accounting and Reporting Practices :** Periodic accounting reports are the most important means of communication between a company and its financiers i.e., shareholders and lenders. There is definitely room for Improving corporate accounting and reporting practice with respect to classification of items in the balance sheet, investment in group companies, intangible assets, and so on.

Index